The MONOCLE
Travel Guide Series

Lisbon

For more information, please visit *gestalten.com*
———
Bibliographic information published by the Deutsche Nationalbibliothek: The Deutsche Nationalbibliothek lists this publication in the Deutsche Nationalbibliografie; detailed bibliographic data are available online at *dnb.d-nb.de*

MIX
Paper from responsible sources
FSC® C011712

This book was printed on paper certified by the FSC®

Monocle editor in chief and chairman: *Tyler Brûlé*
Monocle editor: *Andrew Tuck*
Books editor: *Joe Pickard*
Guide editor: *Chloë Ashby*
———
Designed by *Monocle*
Proofreading by *Monocle*
Typeset in *Plantin & Helvetica*
———
Printed by *Offsetdruckerei Grammlich, Pliezhausen*

Made in Germany

Published by *Gestalten*, Berlin 2017
ISBN 978-3-89955-922-4

© Die Gestalten Verlag GmbH & Co. KG, Berlin 2017

Welcome
—— Head for
the hills

Lisbon may be one of Europe's oldest cities but it's far from staid. In fact there's something decidedly *unruly* about it: massive murals coat tumbledown façades, azulejo-covered townhouses abut cutting-edge museums and those indefatigable yellow trams have the jerkiest of brakes.

It hasn't always been plain sailing (though today, gliding along the *Rio Tejo* is a pleasant way to spend a lazy Sunday). A devastating earthquake in 1755 destroyed most of the city and the global financial crisis left its economy limping. But Lisbon is *resilient*. From the rubble rose a well-planned city, with Haussmann-esque avenues in one neighbourhood and a Manhattan-style grid of streets in another.

A combination of longstanding businesses and keen entrepreneurs has sustained the retail, culture and hospitality scenes. Hotels are responding to the *boom in tourism* with a mix of restored old-world *palácios* and minimalist Scandi-inspired apartments, while commerce is being driven by both traditional tile workshops and sleek homeware boutiques. Lively cocktail bars and modern restaurants are joining family-run *tascas*, while galleries are seeking local and foreign talent. All of the above are facing the future while respecting the city's *intoxicating history*: one bar resides in an old brothel, while a former cod warehouse is now home to a museum.

With its glistening river views and nearby sandy beaches, Lisbon is a *laidback and liveable* city. It's also quietly receptive to new ideas. So take a stroll and soak it all in – with the help of a shot of *ginjinha* and a grilled sardine or two. — (M)

Contents
—— Navigating the city

Use the key below to help navigate the guide section by section.

H Hotels

F Food and drink

R Retail

T Things we'd buy

E Essays

C Culture

D Design and architecture

S Sport and fitness

W Walks

012 —— 013
Map
Get the lay of the land in Lisbon with our handy map of the city, helping you get to grips with the key areas covered in this guide.

014 —— 015
Need to know
From football fans to kissing etiquette, here are some of the basics for navigating the streets and sights.

016 —— 027
Hotels
Beautifully restored *palácios*, contemporary guesthouses and design-savvy apartments: Lisbon has options aplenty when it comes to bedding down for the night. Whether you're visiting for business or pleasure, peruse our guide to the best hotels.

028 —— 047
Food and drink
Lisbon is about more than *pastéis de nata* and *bacalhau* – though we'll show you where to find the best of both. From traditional *tascas* and *ginjinha* bars to sushi counters and Scandi-style coffee shops, we share our favourite spots to eat and drink.

028 —— 039
Lunch and dinner

039 —— 040
Breakfast and brunch

041 —— 043
Coffee

043 —— 044
Food retailers

045 —— 047
Drinks

048 —— 065
Retail
Candlesticks, ceramics and cosmetics: Lisbon excels when it comes to plucky independent shops that specialise in a single item. There are also some top-notch concept stores, alongside idiosyncratic bookshops in which to pick up a new read or two.

048 —— 053
Specialist shops

053 —— 055
Books and records

056 —— 059
Concept stores

059 —— 061
Mixed fashion

061 —— 062
Menswear

062 —— 063
Womenswear

064 —— 065
Homeware

066 —— 068
Things we'd buy
From the finest tinned fish to natty sunglasses and traditional ceramics (plus a wooden sheep), our pick of what to pack from Lisbon's independent designers and signature craftsmen.

069 —— 092
Essays
Tourism, nightlife, kiosk culture and urban art: Monocle friends and family impart their wisdom on these Portuguese subjects and more. Plus, one Lisboeta shares his top tips on how to chow down on sardines without choking.

093 —— 107
Culture
With commercial spaces and art-house cinemas joining the host of public galleries and museums launched in the past decade, Lisbon's cultural capital is on the rise.

093 —— 098
Museums and galleries

099 —— 101
Commercial galleries

102 —— 103
Cultural centres

104 —— 105
Live venues

105 —— 106
Cinemas

107
Media round-up

108 —— 123
Design and architecture
Whether your fancy is for modernist masterpieces, art deco interiors or something altogether more gothic, the cityscape is perfect for a stroll through the architectural styles of the past 1,000 years.

108 —— 110
Visual identity

111 —— 114
Contemporary

115 —— 117
World Expo 1998

118 —— 120
Modernism and postmodernism

121
Early 20th century

122 —— 123
Traditional

124 —— 127
Sport and fitness
Our recommendations for sailing the Rio Tejo, cycling the city's waterfront and finding the sweetest out-of-town surfing spots. Plus, where to spruce up afterwards with a hot-towel shave or a sleek trim.

124 —— 125
Out and about

126
Grooming

127
Cycling route

127
Running route

128 —— 137
Walks
Braving the ups and downs of Lisbon's hills brings its own rewards, from buzzing multicultural neighbourhoods and artsy regeneration to labyrinthine streets and green spaces. Join us for a tour of the cobbled streets – and, of course, our favourite pit-stops along the way.

128 —— 129
Mouraria

130 —— 131
Campo de Ourique

132 —— 133
Marvila

134 —— 135
Parque das Nações

136 —— 137
Alfama

138 —— 139
Resources
Be in the know with our bite-size guide to events, slang and the city's soundtrack, plus hints on what will keep you occupied on rainy and sunny days.

140 —— 141
About Monocle
Find out more about our global brand, from groundbreaking print, radio, online and film output through to our cafés and shops.

142 —— 143
Acknowledgements
The people who put this guide together: writers, photographers, researchers and all the rest.

144 —— 145
Index

Map
—— The city at a glance

Sitting on the banks of the expansive Rio Tejo, the Portuguese capital isn't as small as people often think: the city's outer suburbs sprawl north and west until they meet the seaside villages of Estoril and Cascais.

Lisbon has been charming visitors for more than 3,000 years. It existed in the Phoenician times as a trading port called Alis Ubbo (Delightful Shore) and has had Roman, Moorish and Christian conquerors. But perhaps the biggest influence on its modern layout was the 18th-century earthquake that flattened much of the city. It was rebuilt by the Marquês de Pombal, who created the grid of downtown Liberdade and Baixa. These connect the former fishing district of Alfama and multicultural Mouraria to the east with upmarket Chiado, Príncipe Real and Bairro Alto to the west.

Today, Alfama and Mouraria, with their hilly lanes, ancient churches and small *tascas*, are atmospheric and soulful. Chiado, Liberdade and Príncipe Real are good for shopping, while Bairro Alto and Cais do Sodré are the places to party.

Aeroporto de Lisboa

ROMA E AREEIRO

MARVILA

Museu Calouste
Gulbenkian

Pavilhão de Portugal

AVENIDAS NOVAS

SÃO JOÃO

BEATO

Palácio da Justiça

ESTEFÂNIA E ARROIOS

Diário de Notícias

**CAMPO
SANTANA**

ANJOS

**PENHA DE
FRANÇA**

Museu Nacional
do Azulejo

LIBERDADE E CASTILHO

REIRAS

**PRÍNCIPE
REAL**

Jardím Príncipe Real •

Avenida
da Liberdade

GRAÇA

SÃO VICENTE

Castelo de São Jorge

RELA
APA

SÃO BENTO

BAIRRO ALTO

Estação do Rossio

MOURARIA

CASTELO

Tram 28

**SANTA
CATARINA**

Elevador de
Santa Justa

CHIADO

ALFAMA

SANTOS

Sé de Lisboa

BAIXA

CAIS DO SODRÉ

EDP HQ

RIO TEJO

0   500M   N

Need to know
—— Do as the Lisboetas do

Did you know that you can find your way in the Portuguese capital by using its cobbled hills, party from dusk until dawn and kiss strangers (more than once)? Read on for more essential tips on how to meet and greet, what to tip after a top meal and which direction to head in search of a sandy beach.

Seven hills? I have a perfectly good view from here, thank you

Seven hills
Orient yourself

According to legend, Lisbon is built on seven hills. The origin of the myth is unclear (and there are debates about its accuracy) but the city's slopes certainly contribute to its charm and offer striking views. You can orient yourself by them too. When you're in the centre with the river behind you, the neighbourhoods of Príncipe Real and Bairro Alto are on the São Roque hill to your left, while Alfama and Castelo are on the Graça and São Jorge hills to your right. Baixa, which means "downtown", sits in the valley between them.

Obrigado
Give thanks (carefully)

Most Portuguese are fairly fluent in English and many also speak French and Spanish. They're proud of their multilingual capabilities but also appreciate it if visitors make an effort to speak a little Portuguese. The easiest word to learn is *obrigado* (thank you) – though note that if you're a woman, it's *obrigada*. Never say *gracias*: it's particularly galling to the Portuguese to be mistaken for the Spanish.

What to wear
Best foot forward

If you're exploring the city on foot – by far the best way to get to know it – you'll soon come to realise that seven hills is a big understatement. Steep inclines combined with the city's pretty but precarious cobbled streets mean that comfortable shoes are a must. Lisboetas rarely wear high heels, even on a night out, and they save flip-flops for the beach.

Clothing is equally casual in the Portuguese capital: you won't see many off-the-runway looks here. However, do bring a lightweight jacket or jumper because the breeze off the water means that nights are often cool, even in summer.

They keep trying to kiss me

Greetings
Kiss me, twice

It's normal for men to kiss women when they're introduced rather than shake hands; twice, once on each cheek, is the standard. Men shake hands with other men but sometimes kiss a male member of their own family. Women kiss everyone when first introduced.

Beaches
Choose wisely

With more than 2,800 hours of sunshine a year, Lisbon is one of the sunniest cities in Europe. Its access to beaches is also unrivalled by other European capitals: there are eight within a 30-minute train ride on the Estoril and Cascais coast alone (trains depart from Cais do Sodré).

The problem with the above is that they can get pretty crowded on summer weekends. During peak months you would be better off taking the short drive over the Ponte 25 de Abril to the 15km of surf beaches and bars on Costa da Caparica – a lively resort that's adored by the Portuguese but virtually unknown by tourists – or the picturesque coves of Arrábida. Bus 153 runs from the Praça de Espanha to Costa da Caparica and takes an hour.

Pickpockets
Sticky fingers

Lisbon is one of the safest cities in Europe and major crime is very rare. But the growth in tourism has brought with it a spike in petty crimes, particularly pickpocketing. Be especially careful on crowded public transport to tourist destinations (buses and trams to Belém, for example, and especially Tram 28) and in busy venues such as the riverside Mercado da Ribeira.

It you're the victim of theft, be sure to report it to the police and get a copy of said report if you intend to make an insurance claim.

Gooooooooooool Benfica!

Football
Benfica bonanza

Football really is a national obsession, with everyone from elderly grandmothers to primary-school children avidly following the exploits of their favourite team. In Lisbon, Benfica, who play in red, are – as it stands – the biggest and best. Their 2017 championship win was their fourth in a row and drew crowds of 200,000 to victory celebrations at the Praça do Marquês de Pombal.

The city adversary is Sporting Lisbon and the team also has a long-established rivalry with FC Porto in the north; any match between them is called O Clássico.

Tipping
Little and often

There isn't an especially strong culture of tipping in Portugal but it's polite to leave a small amount in restaurants – usually a couple of euros in *tascas* and cafés and 10 per cent in more upmarket venues. It's also customary to round up a taxi fare.

Nightlife
Late and loud

Lisbon is well known for its bars and clubs, some of which are considered to be among the best in Europe. But the party barely gets going before midnight; if you go to bars before 23.00 you'll likely find them empty. Peak hours are between midnight and 03.00. Most city-centre bars close at about 02.00 but you'll find places in districts such as Cais do Sodré serving drinks until 04.00 – and clubs buzzing until at least 07.00.

When to eat
Midnight feast

The Portuguese like to eat well and regularly. Breakfast usually consists of a strong coffee and a sweet pastry before 11.00. Lunch is from 13.00 (kitchens tend to close at about 15.00) and then come late afternoon, say 17.00, it's time for *lanche*: a snack to keep you going until dinner. It's normal to dine quite late: most people meet for pre-dinner drinks at 20.00 and have dinner at 21.00, although some restaurants serve until 23.00 or even later.

Just you keep on trundling – it's coffee time

Hotels
—— Get a room

The Portuguese capital's hospitality industry is buzzing and, as a result, a crop of charming chains and independent boutiques are springing up across the sprawling city.

Hotels have responded to the swathes of visitors with a shift in quality. A new generation of savvy hoteliers – plus a few canny survivors – offer an array of sleek stop-ins to suit the most discerning global traveller. Sensitively restored *palácios* and centuries-old convents combine history and novelty, while contemporary guesthouses range from eclectic and eccentric to polished and minimalist.

Each and every one of Lisbon's neighbourhoods is unique and the lodgings found within them are no different. But whatever you choose – whether a former apartment block or palace – it will never fail to feel Portuguese.

①
Casa C'Alma, Príncipe Real
Eye for design

Tucked away on the first floor of a pale-pink building, Casa C'Alma overlooks the quiet Praça das Flores. "It used to be an apartment and it still is," says Rafael Reis who, with his partner Sara Madeira (*both pictured*), turned it into a guesthouse in 2016. "Our aim was to create something that feels like a home but pays special attention to detail and design."

The interiors come courtesy of Lisbon-based Arkstudio and combine Portuguese tradition and Scandinavian design. White walls and polished-wood floors make for a clean-cut canvas, which is punctuated with leafy pot plants. The living room has a small library of books and magazines (including MONOCLE, no less) and occasionally hosts workshops and pop-ups.

Each of the five bedrooms has a distinct character and is flooded with natural light. The Suite Deluxe is the biggest and the best.
48 Praça das Flores, 1200-192
+351 919 430 494
acasacalma.com

MONOCLE COMMENT: Casa C'Alma doesn't offer lunch or dinner but there are some great restaurants nearby, including A Cevicheria (*see page 30*).

Santa Clara 1728, São Vicente
Royal flush

Pilot turned hotelier João
Rodrigues (*pictured*) claims
that he went into the hospitality
business by accident. But there's
nothing accidental about this light-
drenched hotel that he runs with
his wife Andreia, which overlooks
the Feira da Ladra. Every fixture
has been carefully considered,
from the freestanding Portuguese
stone baths to the pinewood floors,
handmade tiles and artfully placed
Hans J Wegner chairs.

According to folklore the 18th-
century pile was once home to a
princess. Today, after a renovation
by architect Manuel Aires Mateus,
it's more of an exercise in muted
minimalism than regal excess but
the result is no less enchanting. A
calming palette of grey, beige and
off-white runs throughout the six
roomy suites and the cavernous
reception area, which is lit by a
lunar-like lighting installation by
Davide Groppi.
*128 Campo de Santa Clara, 1100-473
+351 934 418 316
santaclara1728.com*

MONOCLE COMMENT: Most of the
produce served at the 20-seat oak
dining table is sourced from the
Rodrigues family farm in Alentejo,
which is also available to rent.

*Nope, no
fluffy, white
dressing
gowns in
here...*

③
Micasaenlisboa, Graça
Home from home

A prime position at the top of a
steep hill grants this nine-room
guesthouse unbeatable views across
a rambling park to the crenellations
of the *castelo*. The brainchild of
Spaniard Maria Ulecia (*pictured*),
Micasaenlisboa's name reflects
the owner's philosophy towards
hospitality: "There are books and
objects in every room," she says.
"It's as if you are at a friend's house
surrounded by things that have
their own lives and stories."

Pared-back interiors by Madrid
firm Ábaton Architects are pepped
up by Ulecia's flea-market finds
(expect mid-century furniture and
quirky one-off pieces, such as the
sculptural submarine lightbulbs),
as well as her own ceramic tiles in
the bathrooms and sprays of fresh
flowers from the local market.
The experience is ultimately
compounded by Ulecia's personal
touches: homemade breakfast and
leisurely chats over aperitifs in the
small sun-trapping courtyard below.
48 Calçada do Monte, 1100-362
+351 919 090 595
micasaenlisboa.com

MONOCLE COMMENT: Take the
time to befriend Oliva (*pictured*),
Ulecia's spirited dog who has the
run of the communal areas.

Room with a view
The living room overlooks the Castelo de São Jorge

Contemporary hotels

01 Altis Belém Hotel & Spa, Belém: Designed by Portuguese architecture firm Risco, The Altis Hotel Group's boldly contemporary five-star hotel on the Rio Tejo hosts 45 rooms and five suites, a rooftop pool, a spa (*see page 124*), a brasserie, a Michelin-starred restaurant and a cocktail bar. The diplomatic suites have balconies and 360-degree views of the river.
altishotels.com/pt/ hotelaltisbelem

02 Hotel White Lisboa, Avenidas Novas: This monochrome hotel aims to cut through the hustle and bustle of the city. The palette varies slightly in shades of white and grey, fostering a serene setting. The 41-bedroom property has four duplex suites spread across the top floors – ideal for a quick trip to the rooftop pool and bar.
hotelwhitelisboa.com

(4)
Baixa House, Baixa
Each to their own

You would be forgiven for walking straight past this 18th-century block of self-catered apartments on a bustling street in Baixa: there's no reception desk or sign above the door, just a discreet doorbell. Once inside, a sweeping staircase leads to 13 airy apartments, each of which is individually styled and and inspired by a famous Lisbon garden: you'll note the references in the floral Josef Frank wallpapers, framed photographs and cut flowers. Eclectic vintage furniture completes the homely look.

Owner and landscape architect Jesús Moraime was keen to ensure that the rooms were furnished with regional products: cabinets are stacked with Bordallo Pinheiro crockery, blankets are sourced from the Serra da Estrela region and rugs come from Alentejo. Every day, staff restock the fridge with fresh breakfast items such as yoghurt, fruit and cake.
81 Rua dos Fanqueiros, 1100-227
+351 919 090 895
baixahouse.com

MONOCLE COMMENT:
Each apartment comes with a washing machine and dryer (or, if not, a free laundry service), making this a smart option for longer stays.

(5)
The Independente Suites and Terrace, Bairro Alto
Low-key living

Owned and run by Duarte D'Eça Leal and his three brothers, The Independente Suites and Terrace is part of what is becoming a mini empire for the family. It occupies a building next to the Independente Hostel and Suites, opened by the brothers in 2011, and is an altogether smarter affair. The original parquet flooring and stucco ceilings are reminiscent of the building's past life as the Swiss ambassador's official residence in the 19th century.

There are two restaurants on site, Decadente and The Insólito (*see page 46*), where all meals are prepared with locally sourced produce. Plus there's a terrace that's open to the public and ideal for enjoying a glass of *vinho verde* in the sunshine, before heading for a night out down the road.
81 Rua de São Pedro de Alcântara, 1250-238
+351 21 130 2634
theindependente.pt/suitesandterrace

MONOCLE COMMENT: For more from the Independente Collective we recommend Uva do Monte, a 12-room converted farmhouse along the coast about an hour south of Lisbon.

⑥
Palácio Belmonte, Castelo
Secret history

Perched on a hill at the foot of
the Castelo de São Jorge, the 15th-
century Palácio Belmonte is a
listed national monument. Building
work began in 1449 atop ancient
Roman and Moorish foundations
and, in 1640, the private home was
extended into a palace. Then, in
1994, it was bought by ecologist
Frédéric Coustols (*pictured*),
who together with his wife Maria
Mendonça turned it into a hotel.

Palácio Belmonte is a time warp.
Ancient stone busts sit alongside
contemporary works of art and
the walls are lined with more than
3,800 azulejos, which were created
in 1725 and reflect the original roles
of the rooms. "It's about enhancing
the past," says Coustols. And
adding a personal touch: "Here's
a Miró next to a Maria – my wife."

The combination of old and new
continues throughout the 10 suites,
each of which is named after a
prominent Portuguese figure.
14 Pàteo Dom Fradique, 1100-624
+ 351 21 881 6600
palaciobelmonte.com

MONOCLE COMMENT: Opt for the
Padre Himalaya suite in the ancient
Roman tower, which features brick
floors topped with kilim rugs and a
marble bathroom with a sunken tub.

Hit the roof
—
The sleek rooftop offers panoramic views

Ⓗ
Memmo Alfama, Alfama
Something old, something new

Wend your way uphill from downtown Chiado to Alfama, one of Lisbon's oldest neighbourhoods, and you'll find this smart hotel tucked away in a late 19th-century courtyard. Don't be fooled by the narrow alleyway that leads to its entrance: once inside it's all openness and light thanks to Madrid-based architect Samuel Torres de Carvalho's subtle design approach.

The hotel is redefining the standards of hospitality in Lisbon and a night in any of its 42 plush rooms – furnished with high-quality linen, black-out blinds, warm hues and tonnes of wood – will make you feel at home. The structure blends seamlessly with the traditional houses that surround it and historic landmarks such as the Sé de Lisboa are just a stone's throw away.

27 Travessa das Merceeiras,
1100-348
+351 21 049 5660
memmohotels.com/alfama

MONOCLE COMMENT: Sitting on the old Moorish city walls, the hotel's vast terrace will be the highlight of your stay. Enjoy the sunset with a chilled glass of wine by the red-tiled swimming pool.

There, looking suave just in time for sunset on the terrace

⑧
Memmo Príncipe Real,
Príncipe Real
Location, location

Sitting on top of one of Lisbon's
seven hills and offering sublime
views over the bustling Avenida
da Liberdade, this is the third
property from the Memmo Hotels
group. The 41-bedroom hotel
opened in 2016 and provides
guests with an oasis of quiet
in the heart of a thriving retail
quarter, with top-notch bars
and restaurants just a short walk
from their bedroom door.

"We don't have a formula for
a signature hotel," says managing
director Rodrigo Machaz.
"Each hotel is about the place
surrounding it." As such there
are nods to the neighbourhood's
heritage running throughout
the space, including limestone
floors that match those of stately
buildings in the area and a portrait
of the 19th-century prince after
whom the district is named; it's
a simple touch but it works well.

The white geometric building is
spread across four floors, with oak
panelling and green furnishings
adorning the lobby and restaurant
areas. Contemporary pieces of
furniture sit alongside traditional
materials in a comfortable but
informal setting.
56J Rua Dom Pedro V, 1250-094
+351 21 901 6800
memmohotels.com/principereal

MONOCLE COMMENT: The 60-
seat restaurant, Café Colonial,
welcomes both paying guests and
walk-ins, blurring the boundary
between guests and passers-by.

Stay up late
———
The Late Birds Lisbon is set
in a restored 18th-century
building. Tucked away in
Bairro Alto, the 16-bedroom
guesthouse is ideal for those
who want to explore the city
not only by day but also by
night. A mainly gay crowd.
thelatebirdslisbon.com

Palácio Ramalhete, Santos
Literary love affair

This former private palace, in a residential area opposite the Museu Nacional de Arte Antiga (*see page 97*), is an ode to the 18th century: think original handpainted azulejos, polished wooden floors, delicate stucco ceilings and open fireplaces. Don't worry, the overall effect is far from stuffy: the three lounges are peppered with architecture and design books and beyond them is a bright white-walled library.

Each of the 12 bedrooms and four pool suites is different. The Old Kitchen Suite centres on an antique copper-roofed fireplace and retains its flagstone floors, while the Oak Suite features floor-to-ceiling oak panels and chesterfields with river views. Between the main rooms and pool suites is a flower-filled tiered courtyard, leading to a petite pool surrounded by a dark-wood deck.
92 Rua das Janelas Verdes, 1200-692
+351 21 393 1380
palacio-ramalhete.com

MONOCLE COMMENT: Come evening, candles are lit around the pool and a warm glow emanates from the hotel's saffron-coloured walls. Grab a drink at the well-stocked bar and hunker down in a comfy chair.

(10)
York House Lisboa, Santos
Old favourite

This converted 17th-century Carmelite convent took on its current name in 1880, when two women from Yorkshire decided to turn it into an inn. It's separated from the busy road by a zigzagging path of vine-covered stone steps, which leads to a serene patio.

While the labyrinthine corridors are dimly lit, the 33 rooms, which include six junior suites, are light and spacious. Spread across two floors, they vary between classic and modern. We recommend asking for one of the original rooms, which have a certain old-world grandeur and sometimes feature terracotta-tiled ceilings.
32 Rua das Janelas Verdes, 1200-691
+ 351 21 396 2435
yorkhouselisboa.com

MONOCLE COMMENT: Breakfast is served in the ancient cloisters but we suggest taking it out to the leafy courtyard. Lunch and dinner are also available.

(11)
Pousada de Lisboa, Baixa
State visit

Housed in the country's former Ministry of Internal Affairs, this Lisbon outpost of Pousadas de Portugal stands on the iconic Praça do Comércio in the city centre. The 90-room property prides itself on combining luxury with cultural heritage. The 18th-century Pombaline-style *palácio* was refurbished by Brazilian architect Jaime Morais and features high ceilings, wooden parquet flooring and lavish hallways dotted with art that has been borrowed from museums and private collections.

The ground-floor restaurant has brick vaulted ceilings and the kitchen, which is led by chef Luís Rodrigues, is a meat-lover's heaven (with plenty of options for vegetarians too). After dinner head to the outdoor terrace to watch the sun set against the riverside square's canary-yellow buildings.
31-34 Praça do Comércio, 1100-148
+ 351 21 040 7640
pousadas.pt/en/hotel/pousada-lisboa

MONOCLE COMMENT: One of the most luxurious rooms, the Dom Pérignon Suite is where the office of Portugal's former dictator António de Oliveira Salazar once stood. His desk remains part of the decor.

Into the wild — The pool is surrounded by luscious greenery

(12)
Valverde Hotel,
Liberdade e Castilho
In the centre

Opened in 2014 on one of Lisbon's grandest avenues, the vibrant Valverde Hotel combines classic elegance with polished comfort. Its sensitively refurbished 19th-century façade is somewhat inconspicuous but inside is a dimly lit interior that's brought to life with brightly coloured fabrics and eclectic furnishings.

Details such as patterned rugs, 1950s-style furniture, warm hues and both antique and contemporary works of art are strewn across the 25-bedroom townhouse; they can be found everywhere from the small lobby area and reading room to Sítio, the high-ceilinged restaurant and bar. The boutique hotel's prime location is the perfect base from which to explore the city, be it shopping in nearby Chiado or running through leafy Parque Eduardo VII.

164 Avenida da Liberdade, 1250-146
+ 351 21 094 0300
valverdehotel.com

MONOCLE COMMENT: Tucked away from the busy Avenida da Liberdade is the hotel's verdant courtyard – perfect for reclining on a sunlounger with a book.

Food and drink
—— Stepping up to the plate

A few years can make a huge difference to a city's culinary scene. For some time Lisbon's restaurants were limited in number and had a distinctly provincial feel. Today that couldn't be less true. A generation of young chefs has emerged, finding customers in the growing international and tourist population but also among locals who have ridden out a recession and are starting to find that they have disposable income again.

The result is a vibrant food-and-drink sector, with new restaurants and bars opening weekly. Locally sourced ingredients, particularly those whipped out of the ocean, are world-class and chefs are utilising them in innovative ways. You'll find a strong focus on Portuguese fare, with a passion for updating traditional dishes. These modern versions of classics such as *bacalhau* (salt cod) and *arroz de marisco* (seafood risotto) are proving that Portuguese cuisine can hold its own among the most interesting in Europe.

①
Gambrinus, Liberdade e Castilho
Old guard

In the touristy Restauradores area you'll find Gambrinus: an oasis of calm behind a discrete wooden door. With its white tablecloths and besuited waiters, the restaurant, which has been around since the 1940s, is a classic. The service is exceptional and the food is reliably good, with a focus on fresh seafood.

Splurge on the crêpe suzette for dessert. It's made at the table with plenty of flames and flamboyance; a performance that makes the eye-watering €34 price tag palatable.
23 Rua das Portas de Santo Antão, 1150-264
+351 21 342 1466
gambrinuslisboa.com

②

Bairro do Avillez, Chiado
Portuguese provenance

This is the latest restaurant in chef
José Avillez's stable, which now
stands at seven in Lisbon. Skip the
chaotic front bar and head to the
restaurant at the rear. Set under
huge roof lights, it's bright, open
and surprisingly tranquil for such
a large space.

Avillez sources Portuguese
ingredients, including a must-try
blue lobster, serving them with both
reference to traditional approaches
and a much-refined palate. Seafood
and fish predominate – the lobster-
and-crab rice is exemplary – but
meat is also available.
18 Rua Nova da Trindade, 1200-303
+351 21 583 0290
bairrodoavillez.pt

(3)

A Cevicheria, Bairro Alto
Raw pleasures

This small restaurant is one of
Lisbon's most popular. Run by
chef Kiko Martins – who also
heads up O Talho (*see page 39*)
and several other venues – A
Cevicheria, as the name suggests, is
inspired by Peruvian ceviche (but
with a Portuguese twist). There
are pisco sours and plenty of raw
fish, fresh salads and some cooked
dishes such as grilled octopus with
squid-ink sweet potato.

The restaurant's popularity is
its only downfall. It doesn't accept
reservations so you'll almost always
have to wait for a table, often for
as long as an hour (even the chef's
mother has reportedly waited
that long, presumably with more
equanimity than most). If, like us,
you feel that standing on Lisbon's
windiest corner can't be sweetened
by any number of pisco sours,
come early, say 16.00.
129 Avenida Dom Pedro V, 1050-046
+ 351 21 803 8815
chefkiko.com

(4)

Sea Me Peixaria Moderna,
Bairro Alto
Good catch

Portugal's love for fish and seafood
– the country has one of the highest
per capita fish consumptions in the
world – is reflected at this smart
restaurant. You can choose yours
fresh from a wide selection on ice
or ask the friendly staff for their
recommendations.

Dishes are simple, adorned with
potatoes and a small salad, because
the focus is on the quality of the
fish. The space is both relaxed and
discreet and the central location
convenient, making it a good venue
for a business lunch.
21 Rua do Loreto, 1200-149
+ 351 21 346 1564
peixariamoderna.com

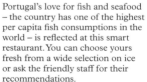

Under the sea

Cervejaria Ramiro is a simple
restaurant in Anjos that serves
an array of fresh seafood
alongside lashings of buttered
toast. The only downside: no
reservations can mean long
queues. Eat unfashionably
early or be prepared to wait.
You've been warned.
cervejariaramiro.pt

⑤
Jesus é Goês, Liberdade e Castilho
Goan, try it

Portugal has strong connections with India and in particular Goa, which was a Portuguese colony until it joined independent India in the 1960s. This colourful little restaurant is a great place to taste the fruits of that connection.

It's an unassuming space, with wooden tables and yellow walls adorned with drawings of Indian gods, but it serves some of the best Goan food you'll ever taste: flavourful without being overly reliant on chilli. The prawn samosas and the prawn curry with ladyfingers are especially good. Take note: it's cash-only.
23 Rua São José, 1150-352
+351 21 154 5812

⑥
Restaurante Bastardo, Baixa
Portugal meets Asia

This restaurant, set on the first floor of the Internacional Design Hotel, has a great location, with windows overlooking the Praça Dom Pedro IV. Its interiors – a quirky mix of mismatched vintage chairs, rugs and colourful posters – are a little questionable but the food is consistently good.

There's a combination of Portuguese and Asian influences such as the *bacalhau* served with aubergine and *kombu* (seaweed leaf). The menu provides wine suggestions for each dish and many are available by the glass.
3 Rua da Betesga, 1200-090
+351 21 324 0993
restaurantebastardo.com

Must-try
Pastéis de nata from Pastéis de Belém, Belém
You haven't properly tried these sweet custard tarts until you've tried them at Pastéis de Belém, which has been making *pastéis de nata* to its own recipe since 1837 and bakes about 20,000 a day. According to Miguel Clarinha, the fourth generation in his family to own and run the business, it's slightly different to most. "The custard is a little less sweet and the pastry is crispier and a little more salty," he says. Of the 50 bakers who work at the site, only three know the secret recipe.
pasteisdebelem.pt

⑦
Café Lisboa, Chiado
Theatrical charm

This graceful space is on the ground floor of Lisbon's 18th-century opera house and its gilt ceilings and old-world interiors evoke the café culture of times past. Along with the dining room, there's also a terrace for summer.

Open from noon until midnight, this is a great spot for everything from a relaxed lunch to an afternoon cocktail or a romantic dinner. Make sure you visit the bathrooms, which are inside the opera house and can offer glimpses of costumed performers rushing through the backstage corridors.
23 Largo de São Carlos, 1200-410
+351 21 191 4498
cafelisboa.pt

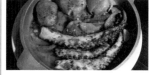

⑧
Antónia Petiscos, Bairro Alto
Warm and welcoming

Bairro Alto can be a tad touristy but, among the bars offering €5 mojitos and €2 pints, Antónia Petiscos is a pleasing exception: a welcoming, cosy space manned by smiling staff who are happy to chat about what's on the menu and suggest wine pairings.

The food is a contemporary take on Portuguese dishes. There's a range of starters: choose several to share and they'll serve as a main course. Menus change according to the availability of ingredients but when they are on offer, the grilled chorizo, cheese boards and mussels in wine are all excellent.
49 Rua do Norte, 1200-050
+351 919 724 122

⑨
Taberna Portuguesa, Santa Catarina
Young at heart

The handsome waiters at this casual and modern version of a traditional Portuguese taverna reflect the ambience of the space. It's a favourite among young Lisboetas, with sharing plates such as mushrooms with coriander and pork with pepper.

Sangria or wine in terracotta jugs are the staples and included in the €30 tasting menu. The space can be a little noisy and the laminated menus aren't particularly sophisticated but the food is good and the service, while laidback, is friendly enough to warm the most critical of hearts.
115 Calçada do Combro, 1200-024
+351 914 289 997

So this is why they say 'packed in like sardines'

⑪
Galeto, Avenidas Novas
Vintage allure

Slightly out of the way, long-standing Galeto is as tourist-free as they come and although the waiters can be a bit forbidding, it's worth a visit for its time-capsule feel: the vintage interior features tan-leather chairs and glittering tiled walls. Order the burger and a beer and imagine yourself back in the 1960s.
14 Avenida da República, 1050-191
+ 351 21 354 4444

⑩
Bistro 100 Maneiras, Chiado
It takes two

Spread across two floors of an art deco-style mansion in Lisbon's upmarket Chiado, the white-walled Bistro 100 Maneiras serves painterly dishes with Portuguese, Yugoslavian, Italian and French influences. Eastern European chef Ljubomir Stanisic opened the 80-seat space in 2010, a year after he began offering an inventive 10-course tasting menu at his more formal Restaurante 100 Maneiras in Bairro Alto.

Start with a thirst-quenching cocktail shaken by bartender Jorge Camilo and moreish potato-skin crisps dipped in herby yoghurt, then choose between updated classics such as grilled squid with zesty lime risotto and pork tenderloin with creamy beetroot polenta. The savvily dressed staff are friendly and the doors are open every day until 02.00.
9 Largo da Trindade, 1200-466
+ 351 910 307 575
100maneiras.com/bistro

Must-try
Bifana from Casa das Bifanas, Baixa
Where the rest of the world has burgers or kebabs, Portugal has the *bifana*: a pork-steak sandwich. Try it at Casa das Bifanas, where the pork is sautéed with garlic and spices. Tastes better than it looks.
+351 21 342 2194

Cervejaria Liberdade,
Liberdade e Castilho
Top hotel table

Cervejaria translates literally as
"brewery" but is often used to
describe a casual dining space,
usually with fresh seafood, simple
traditional dishes and cold beer.
Cervejaria Liberdade, which is the
in-house restaurant at the Tivoli
Hotel, renders this concept into a
calm and sophisticated space with
blue-leather bar stools, polished
wood and large windows looking
out onto the tree-lined Avenida
da Liberdade, Lisbon's premier
shopping street.

Daily fresh seafood, traditional
rice dishes and succulent meat
all feature on the menu, which
also offers a selection of delicate
and delicious sushi and sashimi.
Choose between miniature lobsters
from Cascais, Algarve prawns,
Mirandesa steak and more.
185 Avenida da Liberdade, 1269-050
+351 21 319 8900
minorhotels.com/pt/tivoli

Must-try
Bacalhau à Brás from
Laurentina, Avenidas Novas
It's said that there are 365
ways in which to prepare
bacalhau; *bacalhau à Brás*
– which combines the salty
fish with eggs, finely chopped
and fried potatoes, parsley
and a scattering of olives – is
one of the most comforting.
Laurentina, which specialises
in *bacalhau* and serves more
than 50 versions, is the place
to try it. "The *à Brás* is a classic
dish and ours uses only very
good quality *bacalhau*," says
chef de sala Luís Dias.
restaurantelaurentina.com

⑬
Gulbenkian Café, Avenidas Novas
Museum gem

The café in the Museu Calouste
Gulbenkian's Founder's Collection
(*see page 95*) – not to be confused
with the cafeteria in the Modern
Collection – is under the direction
of chef Miguel Castro e Silva,
credited with being the first to
bring Portuguese cuisine into
a fine-dining environment.

Here Castro e Silva offers some
of his signature dishes, including
the Porto classic *francesinha* (a
meaty croque monsieur), along
with salads, sandwiches and a
good-value €12.50 lunch menu.
The casual space has an outdoor
terrace that overlooks the garden.
45A Avenida de Berna, 1067-001
gulbenkian.pt

14 Less, Principe Real
Less is more

In the heart of department store Embaixada (*see page 58*) is this small restaurant, which shares the space with a bar called Gin Lovers. It's easy to miss – a cluster of simple tables in the pretty tiled courtyard of the 19th-century Moorish-style palace – but well worth hunting out.

Another Miguel Castro e Silva-directed venue, it's no wonder the food is excellent, with high-quality ingredients and well-executed takes on simple classics. The zingy lemon risotto with meaty scallops, the pearl barley with prawns and the braised-pumpkin ravioli are particularly noteworthy. Less is perfect for lunch if you're shopping in the Príncipe Real area but it's also open for dinner, when it has the feel of a peaceful oasis.
Embaixada, 26 Praça do Príncipe Real, 1250-184
+ 351 21 347 1341
ginlovers.pt

15 Bica do Sapato, São Vicente
Star attractions

With a wide outdoor terrace by the river, Bica do Sapato is another firm Lisbon favourite. It's the perfect place to while away a sunny afternoon, watching the cruise ships or checking out your fellow diners (John Malkovich is a co-owner and this is as good a place as any if you're into celeb-spotting).

There's a classic Portuguese menu on offer or you can order from the sushi bar on the first floor. A playlist combines contemporary Portuguese, UK and US artists and the vibe is chic but casual.
Armazém B, Avenida Infante Dom Henrique, Cais da Pedra, 1950-376
+ 351 21 881 0320
bicadosapato.com

Mmm, do I smell seafood?

16

Palácio Chiado, Chiado
Spoilt for choice

It's worth visiting Palácio Chiado
for the building alone, a restored
18th-century palace in the old town
with original ceiling frescos. Spread
across two floors, the space has
eight restaurants and bars.

On the ground floor is a
down-to-earth self-service area
with a bar and food such as steak
and salad available from four
market-style venues. Upstairs is
more sophisticated and includes a
champagne-and-seafood bar and
a delicatessen. There's also a sushi
restaurant, the only space in the
palace that accepts reservations.
70 Rua do Alecrim, 1200-018
+351 21 010 1184
palaciochiado.pt

(17)
Tapisco, Bairro Alto
Dining car

This latest offering from Michelin-starred chef Henrique Sá Pessoa is an informal dining space on the edge of Bairro Alto. Set in a former bakery, the long room offers both table and bar seats and is reminiscent of a (very fine) railway lounge, with industrial lighting and red-leather upholstery.

The name is a play on tapas and *petiscos* (the Portuguese word for snacks taken with drinks) and the menu offers a mix of Spanish and Portuguese dishes, ranging from a very good marinated octopus salad and a sophisticated take on *bacalhau à Brás* to *jamón ibérico* croquettes and squid-ink paella. Designed for sharing, the dishes work especially well when they're paired with the signature Yzaguirre vermouth.
81 Rua Dom Pedro V, 1250-093
+351 21 342 0681
tapisco.pt

Incoming! Just the custard tart I was craving, thank you

Vegetarian

Meat and fish-shunners won't find many options on standard menus but there is a growing number of specialist vegetarian and vegan cafés in the city.

01   **Ao 26 Vegan Food Project, Chiado:** A bit tricky to find but worth it for the lovely space and good-value meals at lunch and dinner. The vegan chocolate mousse is sublime.
+351 967 989 184

02   **Água no Bico, Santa Catarina:** A great option on a warm evening thanks to its pretty, secluded terrace. The portions aren't huge but the ingredients are first class.
+351 910 111 470

03   **Terra, Príncipe Real:** This old-school space, complete with touches of Indian decor and portraits of the Dalai Lama, serves a vegetarian buffet for lunch and dinner. It also has a garden for summer dining.
restauranteterra.pt

04   **Aloha Café, Príncipe Real:** The latest vegan offering in Lisbon, Aloha Café is open for breakfast and lunch and offers an all-day vegan brunch on the weekend.
+351 964 479 474

18

Pap'Açorda, Cais do Sodré
Contemporary tradition

Founded in 1981 in Bairro Alto, this contemporary take on a traditional *tasca* moved to Mercado da Ribeira last year. While the bright new space – designed by Portuguese architecture firm Aires Mateus – is very different, the food remains the same: head chef Manuela Brandão has been with the restaurant since its inception.

The menu features classic Portuguese dishes as well as seasonal specials, with ingredients sourced from the vegetable market below the restaurant.
*1F Mercado da Ribeira, Avenida 24 de Julho, 1200-479
+351 21 346 4811
papacorda.com*

I wouldn't say no to one of those juicy prawns...

⑲
O Talho, Avenidas Novas
Meat feast

O talho means "the butcher" in
Portuguese and this restaurant,
with a small butcher's shop out
front, was chef Kiko Martins'
first Lisbon venue. The space is
dedicated to "the gastronomic
perfection of meat," he says.

Although it uses Portuguese
ingredients, the restaurant has an
international flavour. The tasting
menu costs just under €50 and
includes dishes such as the African-
influenced pork-belly *cachupa*
(slow-cooked stew) with fried corn
and yams, the tandoori lamb and
the Brazilian *picadinho* (casserole).
1B Rua Carlos Testa, 1050-046
+351 21 315 4105
otalho.pt

Breakfast and brunch
Rise and shine

Superstar dining

Lisbon's only two-Michelin-
starred restaurant is Belcanto.
Chef José Avillez aims to
translate Portugal's landscape
into a culinary experience with
dishes such as Wave Breaking,
complete with butter-rich
seaweed sand and a foam that
recedes like waves do.
belcanto.pt

❶
La Boulangerie, Prazeres
French flair

This is the place to come for the
best croissants in Lisbon – and
possibly Portugal. Flaky, buttery
and baked fresh on the premises all
day long, they're worth the visit by
themselves. The pains au chocolat
are also dangerously addictive.

La Boulangerie offers
continental breakfasts – freshly
baked rolls with jam and butter
– and brunch dishes that include
scrambled eggs, smoked salmon
and those croissants again, this time
with unusual fillings such as fresh
figs and soft cheese. The setting
is pleasant but arrive early on the
weekend for a table on the terrace.
42 Rua Olival, 1200-739
+351 21 395 1208

Top 'tascas'

With simple decor and
handwritten menus, Lisbon's
small, family-run restaurants –
tascas – are a reliable source of
good-quality home cooking at
very reasonable prices.

01 Zé da Mouraria,
Mouraria: Delicious
daily specials and a
pretty dining space in
one of Lisbon's oldest
neighbourhoods
ensure that this is one
of the city's favourites.
+351 21 886 5436

02 A Provinciana, Liberdade
e Castilho: Hidden behind
the tourist-focused
offering in Praça dos
Restauradores, this
family-run restaurant is
popular with police and
firemen stationed nearby.
+351 21 346 4704

03 Casa da Índia, Bairro
Alto: Open until 01.00, this
central *tasca* specialises
in grilled meat, especially
chicken. If there's a long
queue you can ask for a
seat at the bar.
+351 21 342 3661

② Tartine, Chiado
Queen of breakfasts

French-influenced Tartine serves brunch until noon on weekdays and 17.00 at the weekends. There's a small bakery at the front for takeaways, or you can eat in.

At €9 and €14, the breakfast menus are expensive by Portuguese standards but include granola and yoghurt along with bread and pastries. You can also order baked goods on their own and standalone breakfast staples such as eggs Florentine and eggs Benedict, which are still difficult to find elsewhere in Lisbon. Staff and menus are multilingual.

15A Rua Serpa Pinto, 1200-026
+351 21 342 9108
tartine.pt

③ Heim Café, Santos
Red hot

This small but pleasant café – think raw wood, lots of plants and wide windows opening onto one of Lisbon's prettiest *bairros* (districts) – serves great breakfasts. The Green Brunch includes avocado toast, eggs and fruit. The Red is a MONOCLE favourite: a sweet waffle with scrambled eggs and bacon.

There are also salads and snacks for other times of the day. Free wi-fi attracts freelance types and, as it's situated opposite the French embassy, you're as likely to hear Gallic tongues as Portuguese. On sunny days (so most of the year) there are also tables outside.

2-4 Rua Santos-O-Velho, 1200-109
+351 21 248 0763

④ Café Tati, Cais do Sodré
Boho charm

Café Tati, just behind Mercado da Ribeira, was one of the first of the new-generation cafés in the city, offering wi-fi and encouraging lazy hours at its tables. The space, with its domed ceiling and boho approach to decor, is peaceful and staff are welcoming and laidback: there's no pressure to move on.

Along with coffee and teas, the café has homemade cakes and sandwiches. It's also open for lunch and evening meals, when boards of cheese and ham make the perfect side to a bottle of wine and the live jazz that's regularly on offer.

36 Rua Ribeira Nova, 1200-371
+351 21 346 1279

Pastelarias

The Portuguese have a love affair with pastries, sweet and savoury, and you'll find *pastelarias* – coffee shops-cum-bakeries – around every corner. They're great spots for a casual breakfast. Try *torrada com manteiga*, a doorstop-style toast and butter, with your coffee.

Coffee
Beans around town

(1)

Hello, Kristof, Santa Catarina
Say hi

This cosy space on Rua do Poço dos Negros – one of the streets that reflects Lisbon's rapid gentrification – bills itself as dedicated to coffee and magazines, reflecting the fact that founder Ricardo Galésio (*pictured, top*) is also a magazine art director.

Along with coffee you'll find breakfast offerings, a selection of homemade cakes and a range of toasts topped with ingredients such as avocado and smoked salmon. There's also a back wall dedicated to international magazines, which patrons are welcome to read.
103 Rua do Poço dos Negros, 1200-336
hellokristof.com

Café com Calma, Marvila
Cool coffee

Until very recently, Marvila in east Lisbon was filled with warehouses and abandoned factories. Much like east London, these large, cheap spaces attracted first the city's artists, then young creatives and now a distinctly cool crowd.

Today you'll find shared workspaces, arts venues, a micro-brewery and Café com Calma: a café that serves coffee, cakes, salads and vegetarian dishes to the neighbourhood's new population. What makes it more charming is that, after the lunch rush, the in-crowd is replaced by grandmothers enjoying a good natter.
10 Rua do Açúcar, 1950-242
+351 21 868 0398

Café A Brasileira, Chiado
Word up

This is one of the oldest and best-known cafés in the city. It opened in 1905 and was a favourite haunt of writers such as Portuguese poet Fernando Pessoa, who apparently liked to drink absinthe and a sweet coffee while he smoked, read and wrote there. Today there's a statue of the poet at his regular table.

Residents tend to visit on Sunday afternoons or late in the evening, when it's one of the few traditional cafés that's still open. Great for a coffee at the bar by yourself or a cold beer and conversation at a table with friends.
120 Rua Garrett, 1200-205
+351 21 346 9541

Copenhagen Coffee Lab, Príncipe Real
Great Dane

Lisboetas fall into two camps: those who see Copenhagen Coffee Lab as a sign of the hipster takeover and those who don't care as long as they can drink its coffee. With white walls, oak counters and blackboard menus, the space offers a distinctly Danish aesthetic along with probably the best coffee in Lisbon. It also has the obligatory cinnamon buns and a menu that includes sandwiches, yoghurt and fruit. It's pricey by Lisbon standards (more than €3 for a flat white) but it's a good spot to chill and work.
10 Rua Nova da Piedade, 1200-298
+351 916 604 054
cphcoffeelab.pt

Food retailers
Bag it up

⑤
Tease Café, Príncipe Real
Sugar rush

Spend a few minutes in Tease
Café and it's almost certain that
you will begin to crave a slice
of something sweet – especially
if the team are in baking mode
and the pretty tearoom is filled
with the mouthwatering scent
of warm, freshly made cake.
Customers are particularly
evangelical about the café's
cupcakes, which are tasty,
beautifully decorated and can
either be eaten in or taken away.

The space belongs to sisters
Ana (*pictured*) and Sónia Cardoso,
who believe a little of what you
fancy does you good. "We have a
big choice of cakes and cupcakes
but there are also salads and lots
of juices," says Ana. A second spot
in Cais do Sodré is planned. The
sister venue will also open in the
evening, offering a healthy food
menu and cocktails.
*15 Rua Nova da Piedade, 1200-296
+351 21 596 2773
tease.pt*

Yes, it can

For about 90 years,
Conserveira de Lisboa has
sold tinned fish: the 1930s
wooden shelves are stacked
with sardines, tuna, cod and
squid. The only problem? The
packaging is so pretty that you
won't want to break it open.
conserveiradelisboa.pt

❶
Manteigaria Silva, Baixa
Odour eaters

Founded in 1890, the original
branch of Manteigaria Silva is a
Lisbon institution and has been
recognised as part of the council's
Lojas com História (Shops with
History) programme.

Its interior remains virtually
unchanged, with marble floors and
floor-to-ceiling shelves. The material
was chosen because it doesn't
absorb odour: understandable
in a shop that's redolent of the
Portuguese staple *bacalhau*. You can
also find a selection of Portuguese
cheese and smoked ham.
*1C-D Rua Dom Antão De Almada,
1100-197
+351 21 342 4905
manteigariasilva.pt*

②
A Carioca, Bairro Alto
Follow your nose

Much like Italians, you'll find Lisboetas leaning against the bar in cafés, knocking back a *bica* (espresso) at all times of the day and night. A Carioca caters to this addiction with rich coffee, which you can smell as you approach the little shop.

It specialises in sourcing beans from Portugal's former African colonies and across South America, blending them to create mixes of varying strengths and flavours: ask the knowledgeable owner to recommend one. You can buy beans, which the staff will grind for you, in quantities of 100g upwards.
9 Rua da Misericórdia, 1200-270
+ 351 21 346 9567

③
Companhia Portugueza do Chá, Santos
Tea time

The Portuguese love affair with tea predates the British obsession – they claim that Portuguese princess Catarina de Bragança introduced Brits to the brew – and Companhia Portugueza do Chá is a strikingly appointed shop in which to explore the relationship.

The space is an old-school emporium with dark-painted walls framed with vintage wooden storage units. Along with leaves from around the world, all artfully packaged, there are special blends including an Earl Grey made with bergamot from Alentejo.
105 do Poço dos Negros, 1200-342
+351 21 395 1614

④
Garrafeira Alfaia, Bairro Alto
By the barrel

This tiny off-licence-cum-bar on the backstreets of Bairro Alto – which sells Portuguese wine, port, Madeira, *moscatel* (a sweet wine that's drunk as an aperitif) and spirits – is an institution. The wine selection changes every 15 days so there's always something new to taste, with the genial staff happy to help you choose.

You can buy a bottle to take away or pull up a stool at one of the tables made from converted barrels and enjoy the in-house tasting menu, with glasses from €3.50.
125 Rua do Diário de Notícias, 1200-143
+ 351 21 343 3079
garrafeiraalfaia.com

Drinks
Raise a glass

Hidden oasis
—
Relax among nature high above the streets

① Park Bar, Bairro Alto
Blue-sky thinking

Lisbon's original rooftop bar, Park Bar, can be tricky to find, situated as it is on the roof of a municipal car park. But it's worth searching for: the lively space has been cleverly converted with low tables and seats separated by plants.

There's a friendly atmosphere thanks to a mix of local and international guests and DJs with upbeat playlists. The bar serves cocktails, wine and beer, as well as various snacks. The west-facing terrace – which looks across the pitched roofs of old Lisbon towards the bridge and the river – is perfect for a sunset spritz.

58 Calçada do Combro, 1200-115
+351 21 591 4011

Riverside and rooftop bars

With the Portuguese capital's sunny climate and sweeping views over the sparkling Rio Tejo, riverside and rooftop spaces are a natural choice.

01 The Insólito, Bairro Alto:
Located on a covered third-floor roof terrace, this small bar and restaurant offers lovely views across Lisbon's old town, castle and the river from hard-to-nab seats on the balcony edge. Come early and in a small group to experience it at its best. There's a good selection of wine and cocktails and, if you get so comfortable that you can't face leaving, there's a small restaurant that's just the right side of relaxed. If you're claustrophobic the tiny lift is challenging but the alternative is three floors of steep stairs.
theinsolito.pt

02 Topo, Mouraria: This unpretentious little bar is hidden away on top of a nondescript building in Mouraria but boasts one of the city's best views of the castle. Take the lift to the top floor and lounge on wooden benches with a laidback local crowd.
topo-lisboa.pt

03 Sky Bar, Liberdade e Castilho: One of Lisbon's chicest bars, situated on the rooftop of the Tivoli Hotel and offering stunning views across the bustling Avenida da Liberdade and the river, this is the place to come if you want to impress your date or to see and be seen.
minorhotels.com/pt/tivoli

②
Pavilhão Chinês, Bairro Alto
Twilight zone

This five-room bar was founded in 1986 and is a Lisbon institution. It's easy to miss, set behind a simple double door that looks more like it belongs to the warehouse that the space once was. Inside, you enter another world, with the walls and ceilings of each room decorated with all manner of ephemera, from toy soldiers and model aircraft in one to diving helmets, mannequins and an entire cabinet dedicated to military caps and hats in another.

Staff wearing red-velvet waistcoats and bow ties serve drinks from a long but traditional cocktail list – the gin fizz is excellent – and other drinks such as tea, coffee and hot chocolate are also available. The back room has a pool table and the whole experience is a little like visiting a wealthy, eccentric uncle's home.
89-91 Rua Dom Pedro V, 1250-093
+351 21 342 4729

③
Cinco Lounge, Príncipe Real
Made to order

This dark, moody bar isn't the most visually appealing space but it serves the best cocktails in the city and its bartenders are charming. Their warmth and the quality of the drinks draw regulars along with discerning visitors.

There's a menu but we suggest chatting with the staff instead: tell them your preferred flavours and they'll make something to your tastes. On a recent visit, a bourbon, whiskey, Campari and chocolate concoction proved to be delectable.
17A Rua Ruben António Leitão,
1200-329
+351 914 668 242
cincolounge.com

④

Rive Rouge, Cais do Sodré
Lights down low

This warehouse-like space on the first floor of the Mercado da Ribeira is an off-shoot of Lisbon's premier nightclub Lux Frágil. Lights are kept low and red pillars contrast with the purple floor.

It attracts a mixed crowd who are less fashionable than the Lux regulars but more diverse in age. The music is the strong point: think eclectic, upbeat old-school funk, played loud. Waitress service at the few bar-style tables is a plus but prices are high for Lisbon (a large gin and tonic costs about €12).
Mercado da Ribeira, Praça Dom
Luís I, 1200-148
+ 351 21 346 11 17
rive-rouge.com

⑤

Pensão Amor, Cais do Sodré
Love and sex

Not all that long ago, Cais do Sodré was Lisbon's sleazy bar strip. Sailors would debark to womanise at bars named after their ports of origin: Liverpool, Tokyo and Copenhagen. Today the area is the hub of Lisbon's nightlife.

Pensão Amor is one of the best on the notorious pink-painted street and claims to be based in a former brothel. Interiors make the most of this salacious history, with an erotic bookshop on site and sexual innuendo throughout. Both the small *pátio* for smokers and the dance floor are always busy.
19 Rua do Alecrim, 1200-292
+ 351 21 314 3399
pensaoamor.pt

⑥

Rio Maravilha, Alcântara
Industrial revolution

Spread over the two top floors and rooftop at creative hub LX Factory (*see page* 60), Rio Maravilha is part restaurant, part bar. The service can be hit or miss but the location, virtually under the Ponte 25 de Abril, has views across the river to the Cristo Rei statue, which the bar mimics with a large sculpture of its own. On the terrace you can enjoy the view and order snacks, along with cocktails and fruit juices. If it's too windy outside there are three indoor spaces.
103 Rua Rodrigues de Faria,
1300-501
+ 351 966 028 229
riomaravilha.pt

Short and sweet

It's a Lisbon tradition to drink *ginjinha*, a sweet cherry liqueur, on a night out – and the premier spot to do it is Ginjinha Sem Rival in Praça dos Restauradores. Here, everyone from older couples to groups of friends sip from tiny glasses in the square outside the bar.
+351 21 346 8231

Retail
—— Bringing the old and the new

Despite the faltering economy, the Portuguese capital is quietly confident when it comes to retail. A combination of age-old companies and plucky start-ups, as well as international and local brands, are showcasing the best of the city.

Chiado may be Lisbon's historic shopping district, along with the luxury boutique-lined Avenida da Liberdade, but today independent shops are prevalent throughout the city's cobblestone streets. Faithful to craftsmanship and tradition, ceramicists and tile-makers are at work in their ateliers, while forward-thinking shops are selling everything from pared-back womenswear and handmade glasses to eclectic homeware and design books.

Lisbon's mix of resilient shopkeepers and lively entrepreneurs has helped lift the mood of a city with plenty to be optimistic about. With friendly staff, a back-to-basics approach, a historic backdrop and high-quality products, Lisbon is open for business.

①
Claus Porto, Chiado
Soap and glory

Founded in the late 19th century, the Claus Porto factory was the first in Portugal to make soap and fragrances. Today the brand is celebrated for its attention to detail (each soap is still wrapped by hand), classic scents and distinctive packaging. This, its first shop, is housed in a former pharmacy and the elegant renovation by João Mendes Ribeiro has repurposed the original wood-panelled cabinets as display units for the extensive range of soaps, fragrances, hand creams and scented candles.

A small room at the back acts as a mini museum, documenting the brand's history, and the smart basement space is a shrine to masculinity: clients can peruse the Musgo Real range and on certain days kick back in one of the Japanese-made barber chairs for a hot-towel shave (*see page 126*).
135 Rua da Misericórdia, 1200-272
+ 351 917 215 855
clausporto.com

②
A Vida Portuguesa, Anjos
Good for gifts

Expanding on the artfully packaged offerings of its original premises in Chiado, this A Vida Portuguesa shop, located in a former tile factory in the artsy Intendente area, opened in 2013. It's the work of former journalist Catarina Portas (*pictured, on right*), who now has four shops in total, including a second in Chiado and a food-focused outpost in the Mercado da Ribeira.

Chock-full of beautiful Portuguese-made products – from port to preserves, soap to stationery, kitchenware to shoes – Portas's alluring shops are unrivalled for souvenir-hunting and personal treats. They also serve as a useful platform for – and for many customers, an introduction to – Portugal's rich design heritage.

23 Largo do Intendente Pina Manique, 1100-285
+351 21 197 4512
avidaportuguesa.com

③
Chapelarias Azevedo Rua, Baixa
Hats off

This Lisbon institution has been
selling traditional hats since 1886,
when it was opened by Manuel
Aquino de Azevedo Rua, a port
producer from the Douro region.
"He moved to Lisbon after a bad
harvest and since all men wore hats
at the time he opened a hat shop,"
says his great-great-grandson Pedro
Fonseca, who now runs the place.

The custom-fitted hats come
in a range of regional Portuguese
styles, as well as classic bowler hats,
berets and caps. There are also
accessories – from printed scarves
to smart umbrellas – to match.
72-73 Praça Dom Pedro IV,
1100-202
+351 21 342 7511

④
Caza das Vellas Loreto, Bairro Alto
Burning bright

Founded in 1789, this cosy candle
specialist is one of the oldest shops
in Lisbon. The Pereira family behind
it is now in its eighth generation
and continues to make everything
by hand in a workshop at the rear.

Dark-wood cabinets are filled
with candles of all shapes and sizes,
from tapered dinner numbers to
stocky pillars and delicate tealights.
They come in an array of colours
and can be made to order and
engraved. Plus, many are finished
with scented oils; you can take
your pick from lavender, rosemary
or pomegranate.
53 Rua Loreto, 1200-241
+351 21 342 5387
cazavellasloreto.com.pt

⑤
Fora, Chiado
Let's go outside

Italian Mazzucchelli acetate frames,
Carl Zeiss Vision lenses and weeks
of handcrafting in Portugal are
what it takes to create each pair of
sunglasses for Fora (Portuguese
for "out"), whose modest, simple
collections belie the lengthy
production process behind them.
Co-founder Miguel Barral, who
started out in the industry selling
vintage glasses, decided to create
the first Portuguese sunglasses
brand in 2013 and make it one
"that others could look up to"
in terms of quality and value.

Fora's new flagship store, with
its striking tailor-made display
cabinet and fuss-free interior, is
designed to ensure that customers
are able to focus solely on choosing
the perfect pair of eyewear. There's
plenty of choice but we would opt
for the honey-toned Goldlover
model, just right for the *praia*.
90 Rua da Misericórdia, 1200-273
+351 21 346 1135
fora.pt

6

Cortiço & Netos, Graça
Piles of tiles

Joaquim José Cortiço spent some 30 years salvaging discontinued azulejos from manufacturers, amassing an enviable hoard. In 1979 he established a hardware shop and soon made a name for himself as the go-to man for tile repairs, often receiving letters from people looking for rare replacement pieces. Today, Joaquim's *netos* (grandsons) – brothers João, Pedro, Tiago and Ricardo Cortiço (*pictured, left to right*) – have injected new life into the business with this smart retail space.

Displayed on simple pine shelves in a pixelated patchwork, the ever-expanding collection now includes more than 300 different patterns and millions of square metres of tiles. Designs range from blocky mid-century geometrics to kitsch floral motifs and are sold both individually and in batches.
66 Calçada de Santo André, 1100-497
+351 21 136 2376
corticoenetos.com

To the letter
———

Livraria Artes e Letras in São Bento is one of those unique places that gives a city its charm. Owner Luís Gomes has furnished the interior with an impressive collection of vintage letterpresses and makes everything by hand, from postcards to illustrations.
arteseletras.com.pt

Luvaria Ulisses, Chiado
If the glove fits

Sometimes size does matter but diminutive spaces such as this traditional glove shop show that charm is still king on the shopping streets of Lisbon. In 1925, when city council executive Joaquim Rodrigues Simões decided to convert his small office in Chiado into a shop, he thought that tailored gloves would be the perfect fit.

"We use the same traditional manufacturing process and have the same personalised service and designs that we've had since it opened," says co-owner Carlos Carvalho. The iconic glove-maker sells sought-after handwear from Portugal and Italy and is renowned for its bespoke service. There's a variety of classic and modern styles for men and women to choose from, with cashmere lining, colourful buttons and contrast stitching as options.

87 Rua do Carmo, 1200-093
+351 21 342 0295
luvariaulisses.com

⑨
Óptica do Sacramento, Chiado
Seeing things clearly

Elegant chandeliers light the way through this luxury opticians-cum-glasses shop, which is more reminiscent of a formal dining room than a shop floor. A short distance from the bustling Rua Garrett, the tastefully decorated and relaxing space was opened in 2009 by optician Rui Romão and stocks a selection of handmade frames from international luxury eyewear brands such as Garrett Leight, Andy Wolf, Cutler And Gross, Stella McCartney and Oliver Peoples.

"Once you've worn luxury eyewear you won't wear anything else," says Romão. We have our eye on the range of glasses from Portuguese brand Paulino Spectacles; the contemporary Chiado model is made exclusively for the shop.

14 Calçada do Sacramento,
1200-394
+351 21 346 2356
opticadosacramento.com

⑦
Burel Mountain Originals, Chiado
Material world

For traditionally handmade Portuguese rugs, homeware and bedspreads, stop at Burel Mountain Originals in Chiado. Founded in 2010 by hoteliers João Tomás and Isabel Dias da Costa, its locally sourced, felted-wool fabric burel is woven on 19th and 20th-century looms in the revived Burel Factory in Portugal's Serra da Estrela mountains.

Staffed by a team of talented seamstresses, the factory offers opportunities for designers to produce and sell their colourful and hardwearing items in any of the brand's three shops (the other two are in Porto and Manteigas). "In the beginning we invited young Portuguese designers to make modern pieces for us; nowadays the designers come to us," says Dias da Costa of the brand's expanding inventory.

15B Rua Serpa Pinto, 1200-108
+351 21 245 6910
burelfactory.com

Top tiles

Solar Tiles in Príncipe Real, owned by the Leitão family, has been trading in antique tiles and Portuguese decorative arts since the 1950s. Sourced from antique shops, the vast collection ranges from 15th-century Islamic pieces to 1930s art deco.
solar.com.pt

Margarida Fabrica, Alcântara
Simple ceramics

Margarida Fabrica, which translates as "Margarida Makes", is an apt name for designer Margarida Fernandes's (*pictured*) ceramics shop. The studio, which she runs with her husband André Melo, makes cups, plates, bowls, vases, and even lampshades for individual clients, restaurants and hotels. Everything is handmade and fired in a small space on the third floor of the main building in LX Factory (*see page 60*).

Usability and a simple aesthetic lie at the heart of Fernandes's work; her pieces are understated and the shapes are organic. "Since the beginning my work has been about functionality; I want to make things that are used every day," she says. "I don't draw my ideas, I create each model by hand and that determines a lot about the pieces and their form."
*105 Rua Rodrigues de Faria,
1300-501
margaridamf.com*

① Livraria Ferin, Chiado
Wise words

Founded in 1840, Livraria Ferin has a distinguished history: it was the bookbinder to the kings of Portugal and in the high-ceilinged downstairs rooms – where regular author readings are held – the original tools can still be found.

The shop offers contemporary novels and biographies along with books about the military, history and genealogy, including some French and English titles. Chat with Mafalda Salema, who has worked here for 20 years and is a font of knowledge, both about the shop's history and the books that it stocks.
*72 Rua Nova do Almada, 1249-098
ferin.pt*

②

Under the Cover, Avenidas Novas
Print prowess

Located next door to the Museu Calouste Gulbenkian (*see pages 95 and 119*), the simple Under the Cover book and magazine shop is an ardent champion of all things print. It stocks an impressive range of international and homegrown titles covering topics from art and fashion to food and travel.

Owners Luís Cunha (*pictured*) and Arturas Slidziauskas pride themselves on being well versed in every publication and its contents, helping guide customers to exactly what they're looking for. The pair opened the shop in late 2015 to cater directly to Lisbon's modern reader. There are many highlights but look out for *Lost*, an annual travel "bookazine" from China, and *The Happy Reader*.

88B Rua Marquês Sá da Bandeira, 1050-150
+351 915 374 707
underthecover.pt

③

Flur, São Vicente
Ambient to rock

"We always try to support local music that connects with us," says André Santos, one of the three partners of this minimalist record and CD shop that has been peddling everything from ambient, club and outsider electronics to rock, metal and African reissues since opening in 2001.

Customers can listen to music before they buy – while looking out onto an enviable river view – with most trusting the owners' discriminating approach to their stock. "We don't like buying in bulk for the sake of having tonnes of records," says Santos. "And we have the same philosophy when it comes to selecting secondhand records as we have for new ones."

Avenida Infante Dom Henrique, 1900-264
+351 21 882 1101
flur.pt

④

XYZ Books, Anjos
Snap happy

This photography bookshop and gallery was opened in 2013 by photographers Tiago Casanova and Pedro Guimarães as a small yet perfectly formed extension of Guimarães' studio-office. Today it is part of a bigger non-profit cultural organisation called A Ilha, complete with studios and an exhibition floor.

Though the pair approach XYZ with a first-timer's optimism, the space is intelligently informed by the successful careers of both. Meanwhile, books are displayed on unconventional and distinctive chunky Nordic pine shelves designed by Casanova.

3 Rua Ilha do Príncipe, 1170-182
+351 916 438 000
artbooks.xyz

⑤
Livraria Ler Devagar, Alcântara
Read between the lines

Housed in the LX Factory
(*see page 60*) in a former print
workshop that once produced the
city's newspapers, Livraria Ler
Devagar takes floor-to-ceiling
bookshelves to new heights.
Thousands of books, ranging from
contemporary novels to historical
non-fiction, line unfeasibly high
walls that tower over the original
printing machines and café below.

The space also has a top-floor
gallery of sorts that displays a
permanent collection of creative
installations made by resident
Italian artist Pietro Proserpio (the
man behind the winged bicycle
suspended from the ceiling in the
main hall). This shop encourages
dawdling with its vast selection of
English and Portuguese-language
titles: its motto, *ler devagar*, is
Portuguese for "read slowly".
103 Rua Rodrigues de Faria,
1300-501
+351 21 325 9992
lerdevagar.com

*I know we encourage
reading slowly but
you've been here a
week now...*

Concept stores
One of a kind

②

Icon, Chiado
Local heroes

Everything in this white-walled shop, run by friends Inês Mendes and Maria Manuel Lacerda (*both pictured, Mendes on left*), is designed and made in Portugal. Detailed drawings by Bárbara Assis Pacheco hang next to Bonjardim soap, leather boots and bags by Labuta, notebooks by Arminho and ceramics from Otchipotchi.

Icon also invites local artists and designers to come and work in the space. "Sometimes people need to be reminded that not everything they buy comes from a factory," says Manuel Lacerda.
6B Rua Nova da Trindade, 1200-303
+351 21 407 3386
iconshop.pt

①

Fabrica Features, Chiado
Bright young things

Four floors above Rua Garrett, this bright shop showcases prototypes and limited-edition pieces by designers under 25 years of age. The inspiring space also stocks a selection of Portuguese items, including Planeta Tangerina children's books, illustrations from Soma Ideas, Serrote stationery and silkscreen posters by Lavandaria.

Fabrica Features was conceived in Italy in 1994 but this is its Portuguese outpost. The spacious shop floor also features an exhibition space for local designers.
83-84 Rua Garrett, 1200-273
+351 21 342 0596
fabricafeatures.com

Ⓐ
Casa Pau-Brasil, Príncipe Real
Brazil in Lisbon

A celebration of Brazil in the capital, Casa Pau-Brasil features some 20 brands from the South American country and is the brainchild of Portuguese entrepreneur Rui Gomes Araújo. "We have many different products here but they all share that one special element: the Brazilian terroir," he says.

The shop is a foray into the Lusotropical imagination, with decorative coconut lamps and a room full of lush plants giving a natural touch. The colourful products on offer in this grand former palace include Granado soaps and Nina Write notepaper, or full-on *carioca* classics in-the-making such as furniture by Jader Almeida. Other highlights include beach bats by Frescobol Carioca, the Poltrona Diz chair by Sérgio Rodrigues and a pretty seed necklace by Maria Oiticica.
42 Rua da Escola Politécnica,
1250-096
+ 351 21 342 0954

④

Teresa Pavão, Alfama
Plates and pottery

This tiny former bakery, home to ceramicist Teresa Pavão's miniature concept store, is a gem for those who favour subtle shapes and clean lines. Her unique and simply crafted objects border on works of art – indeed, she is constantly collaborating with museums and galleries on exhibitions, as well as creating one-offs for some of the city's best restaurants.

The ceramic pieces are made using glazed or polished white clay and often incorporate elements such as bone, iron, silver and even silk. Pavão (*pictured*) also produces a small line of clothing and accessories. Behind the bakery's original marble-and-glass counter is the owner's atelier, strewn with works in progress, where she also hosts workshops.
120 Rua São João da Praça,
1100-521
+351 21 887 2743
teresapavao.com

⑤

Embaixada, Príncipe Real
All in one

The streets of Príncipe Real are lined with shops and several have taken up residence in the grand Palacete Ribeiro da Cunha. Built in 1877, this independent shopping mall – a former embassy – has become one of the most impressive retail destinations in the city.

Spread over two floors and with a neo-Moorish inner courtyard, the grand building invites all who enter to wander from one room to another, exploring the best that the country has to offer. Portuguese manufacturer Urze resides on the first floor, selling wool jackets, bags and throws from Ecolã, a third-generation producer that has been operating from the rural mountain village of Manteigas since 1925. Other highlights include organic cosmetics company Organii, homeware shop Boa Safra and clothing brand UOY.
26 Praça do Príncipe Real, 1250-184
+351 965 309 154
embaixadalx.pt

When shopping, I like to dress for the occasion

⑥
Galerias de São Bento, São Bento
Magical multitasker

Situated on a bustling street,
Galerias de São Bento brings
together a host of goods including
swimwear, modern homeware and
ethical footwear. But that's not all.
"It's much more than a concept
store," says co-owner Grácia Veiga.
"You enter the building through
our shop and café but then you
discover a whole world inside."

The world that Veiga is talking
about has been designed to bring
people and ideas together. In the
same building is a co-working area,
an events space, a restaurant, a roof
terrace and a patio.
25-35 Rua de São Bento, 1200-109
+ 351 912 984 929
galeriasdesaobento.com

Mixed fashion
Twice as nice

①
The Feeting Room, Chiado
Design massive

Already a hit in Porto, this sleek
shop continues on its quest of
promoting edgy Portuguese
footwear with a keen eye for
versatility: JAK's minimal Royal
trainers for women and Freakloset's
multi-toned derbys can be paired
with smart or casual clothes and
are two of the best examples of
"Made in Portugal" here.

The Feeting Room hosts two
mini shops under its arches: one
stocking Daniel Wellington watches,
the other eyewear chosen by "optical
concept store" Clérigos In. It also
sells accessories and homeware.
26 Calçada do Sacramento, 1200-394
+ 351 21 246 4700
thefeetingroom.com

④
Mini by Luna, Príncipe Real
Woman's touch

This attractive shop, complete with a garden, has been treating women and children to the finer things in life since 2012. Owned by Barcelona-born Araceli Piqué (*pictured*), the split-level space combines minimalist Nordic and industrial urban influences.

The womenswear range includes pieces by Pomandère, Anniel, Polder and American Vintage. Meanwhile, from cotton toys and cosy lighting through to Tocotó Vintage baby blouses and Italian-made shoes, the shop is stuffed with charming gifts for kids.
74 Rua Dom Pedro V, 1250-094
+ 351 21 346 5161
minibyluna.com

②
Sapataria do Carmo, Chiado
Legacy on foot

From the cast-iron lettering above the door to the lovingly restored cabinets, this tiny shoe shop has been a treasured part of Chiado's history since 1904. Brands such as Armando Silva and Centenário take pride of place, along with Derby brogues and Oxfords, all packed in individually numbered shoeboxes.

Nearby sister space Shoes You – a venture by four entrepreneurs who took over this former family business in 2014 – sells less formal footwear but is similarly committed to provenance and precision.
26 Largo do Carmo, 1200-092
+ 351 21 342 3386
sapatariadocarmo.com

③
+351, São Bento
Relaxed style

Named after the country's dialling code, +351 was created by Ana Penha e Costa as a tribute to the easygoing nature of her homeland, which she was missing during her time at Rio de Janeiro fashion house Osklen.

Costa's love of sea and surf inspired the casual colour palettes and relaxed shapes of her ready-to-wear collections, which include swimwear. Designed in-house, all her clothing is produced in the textile factories of Guimarães and Barcelos in the north.
18 Rua Poiais de São Bento,
1200-348
+ 351 21 801 5984
mais351.pt

LX rated

Housed in an old fabric-and-thread factory, LX Factory is a creative hub with a co-working space, coffee shops and galleries. There are also a handful of superlative shops: Retroshop for vintage furniture, Pura Cal for homeware and Livraria Ler Devagar for books.
lxfactory.com

⑤
Kolovrat 79, Príncipe Real
Original clothing

"To wear something strong can feel strange but it makes you aware of yourself," says Lidija Kolovrat (*pictured*). "I design clothes for curious people." The Bosnian-born designer, who set up shop in 2010, has long been one of the city's fashion stars and her ready-to-wear collections – each piece unique – defy trends in favour of provocation. Billowy shapes, vivid prints and her trademark leather leaves are all motifs. The shop also stocks jewellery, perfume and accessories from global designers that Kolovrat loves.
79 Rua Dom Pedro V, 1250-093
+ 351 21 387 4536
lidijakolovrat.com

Menswear
Boys' own

❶
Rosa & Teixeira,
Liberdade e Castilho
Sharp suitor

Synonymous with master tailoring for more than a century, Rosa & Teixeira is still the finest spot in Lisbon for menswear, be it a made-to-measure suit jacket or off-the-rack coat. The shop is named after the father and son-in-law duo who started the business in 1915.

The space now houses casualwear and accessories, with a personalised tailoring service on the lower-ground floor. A sculpture by celebrated artist Pedro Cabrita Reis is the only thing in the place bereft of clean, exacting lines.
204 Avenida da Liberdade, 1250-147
+ 351 21 311 0350
rosaeteixeira.pt

②
Slou, Chiado
Setting the pace

André Lima and his friend Alex Vinent set up Slou (pronounced "slow"), close to Teatro da Trindade, in 2013. "We go for smaller, less commercial brands," says Vinent of the pair's collection of sharp yet versatile clothes, which hang on pale-wood hangers in the white-walled shop.

Trusty brands such as Comme des Garçons, Stone Island, APC, Our Legacy and Neighborhood get a look-in. Also lining the shelves are trainers by Common Projects, Adidas and Converse.
22E Rua Nova da Trindade,
1200-303
+ 351 21 347 1104
sloulisbon.com

③
Maison Nuno Gama, Príncipe Real
Famed designer

After years at the forefront of Portuguese menswear, the country's top designer Nuno Gama opened this flagship shop in 2014 to showcase his entire collection, including suits, shirts, accessories and shoes – and often featuring his trademark azulejo motifs and the signature blue that the designer is fond of. Though his runway shows are renowned for their masculinity and flamboyance mixed with national heritage, this contemporary retail space – with mirrored surfaces, soft eggshell walls, gold tones and sculptures by David Oliveira – is more restrained.

Maison Nuno Gama also hosts a barbershop and a nail salon, as well as a private tailoring service for men and women who want to own something personalised by one of Portugal's catwalk kings.
171 Rua do Século, 1200-434
+ 351 21 347 9068

④
Impasse, Liberdade e Castilho
Sporty style

Positioned on a street parallel to Avenida da Liberdade, the city's high-end shopping destination, you'll find Impasse. It specialises in urbanwear and techwear: think skaters and surfers looking for something a little more grown-up and fashion-conscious.

The staff are dismissive of traditional fashion categories – "Our clothes are gender neutral," says one – but men seem to be better served by the selection. The collections are interesting and well chosen, with jackets by hi-tech Japanese brand Nanamica, shorts by Canadian outdoor clothier Raised By Wolves and T-shirts from Laser Barcelona. There are no Portuguese brands to speak of but many of the items are made in the country. The shop also stocks trainers, caps and accessories with a prime focus on sunglasses.
9 Rua de São José, 1150-321
+ 351 21 346 0294
impasse-shop.com

①
Espaço B, Príncipe Real
Watch this space

A precursor to Príncipe Real's high-end retail boom, Espaço B was founded in 2010 and continues to give the neighbourhood's newest boutiques a run for their money. This minimal two-room space features a constantly evolving selection of clothing, jewellery, accessories and books to cater for the most discerning of tastes. It's all thanks to the considered eye of husband-and-wife duo José Luís Barbosa and Leonor Barata, who have both worked as fashion stylists and interior designers.

Kaths Belgium pendants, Tosca Lab designer toys and minimalistic Annette Görtz dresses sit alongside more well-known brands such as Comme des Garçons and Marc Jacobs. The clean interiors and sleek decor allow for a serene afternoon of browsing.
94 Rua da Escola Politécnica, 1250-102
+ 351 21 397 9605
espaco-b.com

② Véronique Boutique, Chiado
Personal favourites

After seven years in London, seven in Paris and stints at Prada and Marc Jacobs, Véronique Laranjo (*pictured*) moved to Lisbon to revisit her Portuguese roots. Véronique Boutique is the result of her decision and, since 2009, the pared-down womenswear shop has offered an enticing mix of refined clothes and elegant accessories.

She only stocks three of each item as "people would rather buy something special", she says. Her delicate edit includes pieces from Vivetta, Markus Lupfer, See By Chloé and Paul & Joe Sister.
1 Travessa do Carmo, 1200-095
+ 351 21 195 2299

③ Fern, Bairro Alto
Fun flair

A promoter of "slow fashion", designer Fernanda Pereira shuns the usual seasonal trends and timetable and works at her own pace to produce comfortable but idiosyncratic pieces that give more than just a nod to her home country. "I work with local producers, which means my collections are limited to a few pieces," she says. "My clothes are more about preserving individuality than the crazy schedule imposed by the industry."

At Fern, jazzy coats made from traditional Portuguese wool blankets, cleverly cut-up geometric party dresses, abstract jackets and a few psychedelic T-shirts (designed as part of label 2nd, a collaboration with her musician husband Noah Lennox) all add to this small space's colourful aesthetic.
195 Rua da Rosa, 1200-384
+ 351 21 347 0208
fernandapereira.net

Check out my new scarf...

④ Galeria Tereza Seabra, Bairro Alto
Bright stuff

Opened in 1984, this shop-studio was the first in Portugal to offer contemporary jewellery. Decades later it's still a revelation: the light-filled workshop in a tiled 19th-century building is a passionate advocate for unique pieces from Portugal, the US, Japan and beyond.

"Contemporary jewellery requires experimentation and that's what we promote," says Tereza Seabra. Her own pendants use materials such as dendritic agate, coral, amber and oxidized silver, and are stunning examples of the art form.
158-160 Rua da Rosa, 1200-389
+ 351 21 342 5383

Homewear
Live with it

① Sal Concept Store, Santa Catarina
Home from home

Interior-design studio Branco sobre Branco has partnered with graphic designer and art director Sandra Nascimento (*pictured, centre*) to turn this former showroom into Sal, a shop celebrating unique Portuguese art and design.

Alongside paintings and collages by local artists, a classic Carvoeiro cabinet, Canavezes soap and Populus wood vases are some of the original products on offer. For those looking for a personalised interior-design service, Branco sobre Branco has more than a decade's experience.
98 Rua de São Paulo, 1200-429
+ 351 916 065 104
sal-shop.com

Best on show

As part of her atelier, designer Cristina Jorge de Carvalho has opened an airy showroom just off Avenida da Liberdade that features pieces from her own furniture line and other brands such as Carl Hansen and Knoll. Visits are by appointment only.
cjc-interiordesign.com

② Verso Branco, Santa Catarina
Well versed

Each piece in this homeware shop has been chosen for its creativity, design and functionality. A high-ceilinged, split-level design shop with a gallery on the bottom floor, Verso Branco has a varied selection of furniture and furnishings, from unique chairs to statement light fixtures and colourful accessories.

Its aim is to bring the designers, the industry and the public closer together. As well as pieces by well-known designers such as Fernando Brízio and Jorge Moita, the shop also works with emerging Portuguese artists and designers.
132-134 Rua da Boavista, 1200-070
+ 351 21 134 2634
versobranco.pt

④ Espaço Mínimo, Chiado
Favourite furniture

"I've always loved architecture and design," says Carla Gonçalves, who co-founded Espaço Mínimo in 2005. Inside her immaculate homeware shop, this passion becomes clear. As well as handling interior-design projects she sells her favourite pieces from the likes of Artemide, Tom Dixon and Classicon.

For something more original see Gonçalves's own collection: her stunning made-to-measure side tables are available in a range of colours, with a choice of teak, birch or oak.

1 Travessa do Carmo, 1200-095
+ 351 21 274 4261
espacominimo.pt

③ Pátria: Arte. Arquitetura. Design, Estrela e Lapa
Cosy corners

By mixing 1950s staples with more modern pieces, owner and architect Euclides Barros has created a small design emporium in the heart of the city. This studio-turned-shop is arranged as a living and dining room, showing off Barros's fine curatorial skills.

Handpicked items include Architectmade toys, Sérgio Rodrigues chairs and furniture from Portuguese brand WeWood, which Barros represents. If you're lucky you might catch one of the nights when the shop turns into an art gallery and hosts exhibitions.

53 Rua de Borges Carneiro, 1200-617
+ 351 21 194 1138

For forks' sake

Cutipol is one of Portugal's most beloved design brands, renowned for its iconic cutlery. Its minimalist designs have a slender silhouette and come in stainless steel, silver and gold. It also has a modern homeware collection available at its flagship shop.
cutipol.pt

Things we'd buy
—— In the bag

The Portuguese capital may not be able to compete with the sleek design shops of Stockholm or the forward-thinking fashion boutiques of Paris but this resourceful city is top of the class when it comes to craftsmanship. Today, over the crest of every other cobbled hill, you'll stumble upon independent designers and local makers turning out high-quality "Made in Portugal" products.

We've handpicked the tastiest take-homes, from sweet *ginjinha* to artfully packaged canned sardines and the creamiest *pastéis de nata*. We've snapped up some summery clothing and sharp sunglasses, as well as an authentic ceramic swallow and vintage graphic tiles worth spending money on. Peruse our sunny spread and pick up the perfect souvenir.

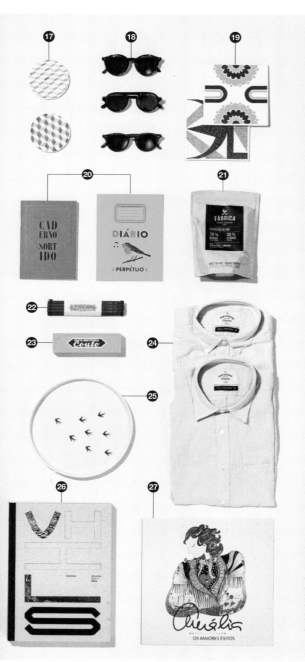

01 So-So wooden sheep from
Loja Quer *+351 966 625 296*
02 Wallets by wetheknot
wetheknot.com
03 Purse by Sul *sul-bags.com*
04 Ana Seixas tote from A Mula
82 Calçada de Santo André
05 Musgo Real soap and
shaving products from Claus
Porto *clausporto.com*
06 Soap by Claus Porto
clausporto.com
07 *Pastel de nata* from
Manteigaria *+351 213 471 492*
08 Bordallo Pinheiro ceramics
from A Vida Portuguesa
avidaportuguesa.com
09 Tinned fish from
Conserveira de Lisboa
conserveiradelisboa.pt
10 Alma Gémea teapot from
Cork & Co *corkandcompany.pt*
11 Bom Dia olive oil from
Mercearia Poço dos Negros
+351 21 138 5681
12 Ach Brito lavender cologne
from A Mercearia Saloia
+351 21 390 1324
13 Esporão wine vinegar from
Mercearia Poço dos Negros
+351 21 138 5681
14 Mingorra wine from
A Mercearia Saloia
+351 21 390 1324
15 Rye IPA by LX Brewery
lxbrewery.pt
16 Ginja by Ginjinha sem Rival
+351 21 346 8231
17 H.a.n.d. ceramic coasters
from Icon *iconshop.pt*
18 Sunglasses by Fora
fora.pt
19 Vintage tiles from Cortiço
& Netos *corticoenetos.com*
20 Serrote notebook and diary
from A Vida Portuguesa
avidaportuguesa.com
21 Coffee by Fábrica
fabricacoffeeroasters.com
22 Viarco pencils from
A Vida Portuguesa
avidaportuguesa.com
23 Couto toothpaste from
A Vida Portuguesa
avidaportuguesa.com
24 Portuguese Flannel shirts
from Slou *sloulisbon.com*
25 Plate by Margarida Fabrica
margaridamf.com

26 *Ephemera* Vhils monograph by Miguel Moore from Underdogs Art Store
under-dogs.net

27 *Amália: Os Maiores Êxitos* vinyl by Amália Rodrigues from Discoteca Amália
+351 21 342 0939

28 *Lisbon Poets* by Luís Camões from Apaixonarte
apaixonarte.com

29 *Capital* by Afonso Cruz from Livraria Ler Devagar
lerdevagar.com

30 T-shirts by +351
mais351.pt

31 Coração wood polish from A Vida Portuguesa
avidaportuguesa.com

32 Lisboa map by Lisbon Sustainable Tourism from A Mula
82 Calçada de Santo André

33 Galache olive oil from A Mercearia Saloia
+351 21 390 1324

34 *Vazio* by Catarina Sobral from Livraria Ler Devagar
lerdevagar.com

35 Print by Mariana a miserável from Ó! Galeria
ogaleria.myshopify.com

36 Blanket by Burel Mountain Originals *burelfactory.com*

12 essays
—— Letters from Lisbon

1
History lesson
Lisbon's colonial past
Syma Tariq,
writer

2
Sensing spaces
Architecture and design
Anna Winston,
writer

3
Nice to eat you, Lisbon
The one-day diet
Tiago Pais,
writer

4
Talk of the Tejo
A river runs through it
Trish Lorenz,
Monocle

5
Writing's on the wall
Urban art
Chloë Ashby,
Monocle

6
Fresh start
Portugal's self-rediscovery
Pedro Santos Guerreiro,
editor in chief of 'Expresso'

7
Nightlife Midas
A new patron saint
Joana Stichini Vilela,
writer

8
Creating a scene
Cultural revolution
Mariana Duarte Silva,
director of Village
Underground Lisboa

9
Let's get together
Kiosk culture
Carlota Rebelo,
Monocle

10
Avian allure
Portugal's swallows
Josh Fehnert,
Monocle

11
Fishy business
Sardines as culinary icon
Luís Leal Miranda,
writer

12
Heart's desire
Hooked by 'saudade'
Anja Mutic,
writer

Now this is what I call holiday reading

ESSAY 01
History lesson
Lisbon's colonial past

———

Today the Portuguese capital is particularly humming with tourists and residents – but its intermingling of cultures and characters is nothing new.

by Syma Tariq, writer

Culture, as Amílcar Cabral once put it, is simultaneously the fruit of a people's history and a determinant of it. One of Africa's foremost anti-colonial leaders, Cabral never lived to see his twin homelands of Cape Verde and Guinea-Bissau gain independence from Portugal in the mid-1970s, when the fight for liberation ended across Lusophone Africa with the fall of the fascist regime. If Cabral were to visit Lisbon today, however, perhaps he'd feel a sense of vindication.

The city, a draw for millions who bank on its sunny welcome and deference to outsiders, depends on its colonial past for its cultural capital. Lisbon's contemporary cool can be framed by a long history of multiple occupations and expansion, from the spice and slave trade during the heyday of the Discoveries that funded its greatest monuments to the Angolan financiers who propped it up after the 2010 crisis. Then there are the imported workers who have been tap-tap-tapping

away at its cobblestones and the young bedroom producers of techno-inflected *batida*, heard in nightclubs from London to Tokyo. Lisbon is an intriguing blend of stories that begins way before what is normally defined as the globalised era.

The Phoenicians were the first to spot an opportunity on the mouth of the glittering Tejo estuary, turning an indigenous settlement into a trading hub that many have wanted a piece of ever since. The patchwork urbanism of these seven hills reveals how these successors have, in one way or another, left their mark. Duck into the underground Roman galleries downtown (sadly only open two days a year) and witness a subterranean world of tunnels, vaulted avenues of water and mysterious nooks exposing the ruins of a city egotistically renamed by Caesar as Felicitas Julia.

Or walk around the charming, Google Maps-defying maze that constitutes Alfama, with its winding lanes and resilient Moorish walls, to discover the Al-Ishbuna that North African settlers called home for more than 400 years – until the conquistadors finally laid claim after numerous foiled attempts. Helped by English, Flemish, German and French crusaders, the bullish Afonso Henriques then declared himself the country's first monarch in 1143. Of the many cathedrals built by his enlarged Christian kingdom, perhaps Igreja de São Domingos – with its blackened walls, pockmarked pillars and restructured salmon-pink ceiling – is the most profound architectural example of Lisbon's tumultuous history: the church has survived two earthquakes and a fire.

From the 15th century – when Vasco da Gama broke the Venetian monopoly on eastern trade with a new route towards India, and Pedro Álvares Cabral's hardy fleet conquered Brazil – the Portuguese capital, with its sights firmly set outwards, became one of the richest cities in Europe. As a catalyst for the Atlantic slave trade thanks to shipbuilding innovations and the demand for labour, gold, sugar and coffee in the growing new world, the city was awash with spoils of expansion, while African slaves became a common sight in its alleyways. By the early 19th century, Portugal ruled several African outposts, including the islands of Cape Verde and São Tomé and Príncipe, and the coastal nations of Angola, Mozambique and Guinea-Bissau.

During the 20th century the dictatorship of António de Oliveira Salazar, said to have distracted its people through "football, fado and Fátima", renamed its colonies as "provinces" – linguistically reinforcing these faraway settlements as part of Portugal itself. Many Lisboetas will tell you that theirs is not a classic tale of European colonialism: intermingling was encouraged and the empire focused more on occupation than oppression. The details are more brutal, of course, though Lisbon's sensory panorama might make it easy to forget them: the heady scent of *calulu* (fish-and-spinach stew) wafting from a São Toméan kitchen window, or the *kizomba* (Angolan pop music) rhythms blaring from a chain supermarket. Angolan bankers now casually window-shop in Avenida da Liberdade. Posters with Afro-style motifs advertise exhibitions and conferences, suggesting a multicultural moment that goes way beyond football, fado and Fátima.

"Lisbon's contemporary cool can be framed by a long history of multiple occupations and expansion"

Leave the centre and the narrative of a prosperous cosmopolitanism reveals a few cracks. From 1974 onwards, a wave of migrants from the former colonies came to the capital, mostly working on EU-supported construction projects and living in almost entirely African-populated suburbs. It's from these outskirts that some of the best dance music in the world now originates but they are a world apart from the sunny start-up prosperity happening a few metro stops away. After decades of stigma, neglect and segregation, unresolved issues remain: a campaign to overturn a law denying citizenship to some Afro-descendants born and raised here is yet to prove fruitful, for example. As tourism rises inexorably, with the world absorbed once again by this polyglot city, now could be the time for some candid reflection.

As Lisbon relies on its reputation as a centuries-old melting pot to attract international tourists and investors, its post-crisis rise from the ashes heralds a success story that other cities now envy. But some critics have also likened Lisbon's tourism-related boom to the earthquake that completely destroyed the city in 1755. Although the merchant classes found their feet again after that cataclysm, with the majestic (and apparently, still earthquake-proof) downtown quarter of Baixa rebuilt by the Marquês de Pombal, thousands were pushed out.

Like the wild Atlantic Ocean that helped make it what it is, Lisbon is no stranger to turbulence and change. But one thing is certain: its penchant for mixing it up will continue to determine its history. — (M)

Afro-Portuguese artists

01 Délio Jasse
Photographer and producer of experimental prints.
02 Mia Couto
Novelist blending Portuguese and Mozambican styles.
03 DJ Marfox
Pioneer of the *batida* club sound.

ABOUT THE WRITER: Syma Tariq is a journalist, radio producer and researcher who works in Portugal, the Maghreb and south Asia. Her heart has been dragged back to Lisbon innumerable times since 2010 – mainly due to its beaches and plucky music scenes.

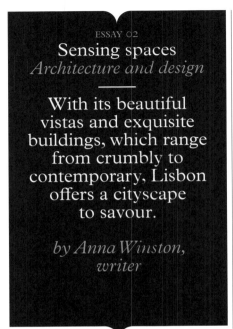

Sensing spaces
Architecture and design

With its beautiful vistas and exquisite buildings, which range from crumbly to contemporary, Lisbon offers a cityscape to savour.

by Anna Winston, writer

Lisbon rewards the leisurely visitor, the slow walker, the ambler. It's almost impossible to rush anywhere anyway thanks to the steep inclines that wait around every other corner and the narrow, irregular streets that can make simple taxi journeys feel off-road. Even the trams take their time and the famous number 28 tends to be so packed that it's tough to get on. The metro may offer some useful shortcuts and easy access to some of the best examples of modern architecture outside of the historic centre but a walk through town with no set route, no fixed arrival time and a bit of flexibility about your destination will arguably yield the richest rewards.

Highlights of an off-the-cuff amble include the streets of Chiado, a wealthy district rebuilt following a fire in the 1980s. The revamp was courtesy of Portuguese architect Álvaro Siza Vieira, a legend in his own lifetime with a reputation for quietly perfect buildings. Then there's the multistorey car park that has a rooftop bar (*see page 45*), the Escher-like stairs and funicular railway of Bica and the views of the Rio Tejo that appear over hills.

Open shutters might offer a glimpse of the city's new wave of contemporary interior architecture, which mingles traditional Portuguese materials such as the distinctive encaustic tiles with pure white walls,

"Dawdling could easily be Lisbon's official sport and the 'miradouros' bring tourists and residents together in its pursuit"

cooling concrete and clever spatial arrangements. Or they might reveal some of the problems facing the city as it becomes the focus of more foreign interest: the Airbnb-ification of the centre and a particularly pernicious form of façadism that sees buildings stripped of everything that makes them unique inside to satisfy the desire for newness on the contemporary property market.

You might wander the cobbles of Baixa, the city centre, rebuilt on a partially pedestrianised grid by the Marquês de Pombal. Or the twists and turns of Alfama, where there is still a vague suggestion of its Moorish past if you squint. But the real defining feature of the city is not the grid or the almost ridiculous grandiosity of the Praça do Comércio. It's not the hidden 1960s concrete glory of the Museu Calouste Gulbenkian (*see pages 95 and 119*), designed by Pedro Cid, Ruy Jervis d'Athouguia and Alberto Pessoa, the bling baroque church interiors or the splendour of the 17th-century Palácio Azurara, home to the museum of Portuguese decorative arts. It's the *miradouros*: the lookout points scattered around the hills of the old town.

These public spaces, with their all-day lounging, late-night drinking and busking of varying degrees of quality, sometimes feel like the soul of the city and certainly offer the best views of it. The first one I stumbled upon, and still my favourite, is the Miradouro de Santa Catarina. By mid-afternoon it's usually bustling with people from all walks of life.

Dawdling could easily be Lisbon's official sport and the *miradouros* bring tourists and residents together in its pursuit. In Lisbon, public space is where life happens. And this is why Lisbon's first major new building in decades, the Maat (*see pages 94 and 112*) designed by UK architect Amanda Levete, has found such rapid success, despite being on a

Contemporary Portuguese architects

01 Fala Atelier
Responsible for world-class apartment refurbishments.
02 Barbas Lopes Arquitectos
Leading the way in thoughtful architectural resuscitation.
03 Álvaro Siza Vieira
Exercises a pure but playful approach to form making.

difficult-to-reach site on the industrial waterfront, separated from the city by a major road.

The building's undulating roof terrace offers a fresh kind of *miradouro* and a gentle new hill in the city's topography. "The public spaces, the democratic roofscape offering spectacular views of Lisbon and the steps down to the river are as important as the building itself," says Levete. "We wanted people to appropriate the building and feel able to walk over, under and through it, blending structure into landscape."

Lisbon was, for a long time, a point of departure; a gateway from Europe to the rest of the world. The Maat represents a new phase in its life, a place that is finding a new expression of itself and should be visited in its own right – but with dawdling still very much encouraged. — (M)

ABOUT THE WRITER: Anna Winston is a design writer and editor who contributes to publications such as *Oak: The Nordic Journal* in Denmark and *Icon* in the UK. Born and bred in London, she splits her time between various cities in Europe.

ESSAY 03

Nice to eat you, Lisbon
The one-day diet

___

What happens when a well-intentioned doctor tells a 'tasca' addict to avoid his city's most traditional and delicious dishes – and desserts too? One hungry Lisboeta dishes the dirt.

*by Tiago Pais,
writer*

"*Tasca*" is a small word that saves us Portuguese speakers a lot of trouble when it comes to describing cheap, no-frills restaurants that serve hearty, homemade meals. In 2016 I published a book about such establishments. My plan was to write a small guide listing my favourites and call it *Lisbon's Tasca Guide*. But my editor told me to aim higher and choose the 50 best in Lisbon. Being a jobless journalist I didn't argue, I ate. If I was going to make such a bold statement on the cover – *tascas* are serious business – I had to try at least 100.

When I finished eating and writing I went to the doctor for a check-up. I wasn't feeling sick; surprisingly, I hadn't even gained weight. Instead I had just been awarded a permanent contract and with it came free health insurance.

After opening the envelope containing my test results, the doctor asked me whether there had been any changes to my diet over the past year. "Well, I tried more than 100 *tascas* in less than six months."

She nodded and explained that some of my results were abnormal. Nothing serious, she told me, while advising me to keep a safe distance from desserts and the tempting dishes that *tascas* usually serve.

At first I thought it would be easy to respect her advice. Like many other cities, Lisbon has seen an influx of no-fat, low-carb, gluten-free places and some of them are actually pretty tasty. Also, I was allowed to eat grilled fish. But my first challenge came on my way back to work. As I was passing A Manteigaria, my favourite place for *pastéis de nata*, I heard the bell announcing a fresh batch and could smell the hot, buttery pastry. No more than 15 minutes had passed since I'd left the doctor's and I was already thinking to myself: just this one, it won't kill you.

I resisted valiantly – crossing the street is always a good tactic – but things got worse once I got to work. "Hey, Tiago. Got any lunch plans? I want to try that *bitoque* you keep raving about." Any other day that email would have made me salivate. A *bitoque* is a *tasca* classic: steak topped with a fried egg and served with chips. What makes it special is the sauce: a magical blend of pork fat, garlic and bay leaves, and white wine or beer.

"This egg obsession is God's fault: the nuns used the whites when ironing their habits and the monks used them to filter wine"

I politely refused. Did I feel strong and resolute? No, just hungry. I had lunch alone at a nearby restaurant, where instead of *cabidela* (chicken rice cooked in its own blood) or *bacalhau à Brás* (cod scrambled with eggs and chips), I ordered grilled salmon with salad. The waiter asked if I was saving myself for dessert: *abade de priscos*, a pudding made with more than a dozen egg yolks, Port wine and pork belly. After lunch I skipped my usual coffee at the nearby pastry shop: I couldn't bear to look at another custard tart. This egg

ESSAY 04

Talk of the Tejo
A river runs through it

Once a point of departure for adventurers in the 15th and 16th centuries, the Rio Tejo is now a destination for cyclists, runners, drinkers and diners.

by Trish Lorenz, Monocle

obsession is technically God's fault: the nuns used the whites when ironing their habits and the monks used them to filter wine. When sugar cane arrived from Madeira and Brazil they created sweet recipes with the remaining yolks. In other words, a miracle happened.

That night I had dinner plans with some fellow journalists – we were trying out a new restaurant – so I used it as an excuse to end all this nonsense. Still, I kept fasting until dinner. I shouldn't have: the chef at this joint was influenced by René Redzepi and the New Nordic cuisine. This meant lots of leaves, pickled radishes, broad beans, celeriac, baby carrots, wildflowers and not a pinch of what I was craving. What the doctor should have prescribed was a stint in Denmark.

The next day I had bacon, eggs and a *pastel de nata* for breakfast. I ate a *bitoque* for lunch and washed it down with a beer. I didn't skip dessert, nor coffee with an egg-filled pastry. I had *bacalhau à Brás* for dinner. I also walked a lot between meals and did the same over the following weeks, with the occasional visit to the gym. Six months later, I returned to the doctor and repeated the tests. Crystal clear. — (M)

ABOUT THE WRITER: Lisbon-born Tiago Pais eats and writes – and often writes about what he eats, mainly for digital newspaper *Observador*. He has also written a book called *The 50 Best Tascas in Lisbon*.

The Rio Tejo runs through Lisbon like a broad blue ribbon. By the time it reaches the city it's virtually at the sea and it's wide and majestic. You catch glimpses of it sparkling in the sunshine throughout the day, sometimes at the most unlikely moments: on a tram ride as you rattle up a hill, from a friend's kitchen window while you wash the dishes or on a walk to the shops as you turn a corner on one of the higher roads.

To me the river is emblematic of the city. I chose both of the apartments I've lived in here because of the river views that they offered. Drinking a coffee on the balcony in the morning, watching the creamy wakes of the small red commuter ferries crisscross the deep blue water still makes me feel, four years later, as if I'm on a permanent holiday. Flying back into the city, the sight of the river and its red-iron bridge signifies that I'm home. If I'm away, I miss its briny scent and the sound of container-ship foghorns on winter mornings.

Historically the Tejo, or Tagus as it's known in English, has played a vital role in the development of the city. As the poet Fernando Pessoa put it: "There navigates in it still, for those who see what's not there in everything, the memory of fleets."

Fleets of ships have sailed the Tejo's waters since the time of the Phoenicians. Fishermen and traders plied their craft here and in the 15th century Portugal's explorers set sail from the river's banks, discovering Brazil and parts of Africa and opening trade routes to India. Until the mid-20th century, the Tejo was at the heart of the city's economic growth and contributed to its diverse and multicultural population.

But in more recent times Lisbon has turned its back on the water. For decades during the second half of the 20th century, the Tejo was nothing more than a pathway for container ships and ferries. Its banks became industrial, neglected and separate from the city. A four-lane road and two-line railway to the coastal towns were built along its bank and still thrum with traffic. Carparks took over the riverside squares; there were no footpaths, few restaurants and, aside from a handful of hardy anglers, the people who lived alongside the river largely chose to ignore it.

But by the start of the 21st century things began to change. A restaurant area emerged in the shadow of the bridge, the sound

"The river has re-entered the city's consciousness and a promenade along its banks on a sunny afternoon is becoming a ritual"

of traffic a constant though not entirely unpleasant hum as you dine. Underground clubs began to make use of former warehouses and a nightlife of sorts emerged: dark, damp and a little grungy but with zingy music and dancing that continued into the early hours.

Then the tourists began to arrive and kept arriving, drawn to the river, its ever-changing colour and the pleasure of being beside a body of water on a hot sunny day. At first Lisboetas looked askance at this passion for the brackish scents and industrial spaces but slowly they too began to reappreciate the Tejo's charms.

The council kickstarted things with investment in a riverside esplanade and cycle path, a new park, street furniture and an expansion of the cruise port. Huge 12-storey white ships now glide daily under the bridge, docking at the far end and disgorging their human cargo. Sailboats have reappeared on weekends, tiny handkerchiefs of white bobbing in the wake of ferries and ships.

Enterprising locals followed suit, opening bars, kiosks and restaurants on the former docks and piers. At one, near Cais do Sodré, you can sit in a deckchair, drink a cold beer and listen to live music as the water flows past your feet. At the Belém end of the city the Maat (*see pages 94 and 112*) rises like a pale wave beside the water and around it street food, music and performance bud and blossom. On Wednesday nights in the summer, tango dancers take over the outdoor riverside auditorium at the nearby Champalimaud Centre for the Unknown (*see page 111*) to dance beside the silver moonlit water.

Challenges remain. Accessing the waterfront still means negotiating the main road and railway and there are only four or five places where it's possible to

safely cross. And in some ways the Tejo still acts as a barrier: most Lisboetas rarely visit the opposite banks. Perhaps they'll take a ferry across to Cacilhas for fresh seafood and a glass of Portuguese sparkling wine on a warm Sunday evening but they know little of towns such as Barreiro and Seixal, dormitory suburbs for those who work in the city but can't afford to live in it.

But the river has re-entered the city's consciousness and a promenade along its banks on a sunny afternoon is becoming a ritual. The Tejo's slow metamorphosis is also reawakening the collective memories and dreams that the beauty and tranquillity of a wide river can inspire in people. Pessoa's words, which decorate the river's bike paths and walkways, sum it up: "Through the Tejo you go to the world." — (M)

ABOUT THE WRITER: Trish Lorenz is MONOCLE's Lisbon correspondent and has lived in the city for four years. She intended to spend only three months here but the sunshine, water and laidback lifestyle seduced her into moving permanently.

Writing's on the wall
Urban art

———

From spidery graffiti to awe-inspiring murals, urban art has long played a role in the regeneration of this city. We brush up on the public art scene and its key players.

by Chloë Ashby, Monocle

From baroque to Basquiat and Banksy wannabes, the neighbourhoods of Lisbon are brimming with art: glistening azulejos, breathtaking murals and massive scrawls of in-your-face graffiti. "City streets are the world's greatest museums," says Portugal's most famous urban artist Alexandre Farto (otherwise known as Vhils). But what makes his city unique and how has public art driven its regeneration?

Before the earthquake of 1755, Lisbon was awash with bright-white walls; afterwards the more affluent areas assumed a lick of colour and a smattering of decorative tiles – and run-of-the-mill graffiti became prolific in the poorer parts of town. Fast forward to the Carnation Revolution in 1974 and the desire for self-expression grew. Graffiti gave artists a chance to tell a story.

In 2008 city hall initiated a programme to wipe clean the façades of the most visible streets, particularly in the historic neighbourhood of Bairro Alto, which by then was plastered with stencils and tags. At the same time, however, it established the Galeria de Arte Urbana (Gau) to manage urban art in the city and legalise other areas for artistic intervention. Ever since, Lisbon has adopted a progressive strategy that supports urban art and makes certain abandoned buildings readily available to artists. It recognises that good-quality public art can be an asset – and Vhils' minutely detailed relief portraits, which are etched and carved into the crumbling façades of neglected properties, are just one example.

So how do you define what's good quality? Can you draw a line between graffiti and urban art? Though Vhils would argue that graffiti is important to a city's identity, many see it as unsightly vandalism that speaks only to a closed community. Urban art, on the other hand, communicates with a wider public. And since it's legal, artists have the opportunity to put more time and thought into it and to create something bigger and better.

"Artists draw inspiration from the jumble of materials, colours, periods and textures; their creations, which are both astonishingly big and curiously small, add to the melange"

Stroll down Avenida Afonso Costa in Areeiro and you'll see what I mean. Polish artist Przemek Blejzyk's "Crossroads" is a towering mural of a frail old lady that he painted on the façade of a 10-storey building in 2015. She's about to cross the road with a dog and a goose, wearing a levitating hat with bunny ears and smoking a slender cigarette with all the elegance of a Parisian. Blejzyk, also known as Sainer, took the faded yellow of the building as his backdrop, while his subject was (to an extent) inspired by the busy location.

Lisbon is a natural – and increasingly popular – canvas for artists. Alongside the pastel buildings, terracotta roofs and cobbled streets, the city abounds with derelict buildings that have boarded-up windows and tumbledown walls. Artists draw inspiration from the jumble of materials, colours, periods and textures; their creations, which are both astonishingly big and curiously small, add to the melange. Of course, the sunny weather also helps: painting in the rain would just be miserable.

City hall isn't the only official party involved. Another organisation helping artists to paint legally is Underdogs (*see page 101*), a multifaceted cultural platform founded by Vhils in 2010. While Gau finds the walls and oversees the permits, Underdogs takes care of the rest: inviting artists from both home and abroad, sorting out logistics, buying materials and booking that all-important cherry-picker.

Urban art animates rundown and forgotten areas. "Most of the murals are painted on abandoned buildings and that creates not only a new way in which to see those buildings but also an awareness of them," says Portuguese artist Angela Ferreira, known in the art world as Kruella D'Enfer. For her, urban art brings to light the city's state of decay. Rather than simply making their mark on a building, these artists want their site-specific works to be a part of it. "Instead of adding to a wall, I'm extracting – making what's invisible visible," says Vhils, who creates

his lifelike portraits by carefully chiselling away at the surface with electric hammers and drills.

As well as exposing layers of history, urban art can shape the future. Lisbon differs from one neighbourhood to the next and, just as artists draw from the jumbled cityscape, they're inspired by these social irregularities. Urban art has the power to change a neighbourhood's outlook: "It's 100 per cent exposure," says Ferreira. It draws attention to previously ignored parts of the city and encourages exploration. "It also creates a dialogue between creatives and the city," adds her partner Pedro Campiche, also known as AkaCorleone.

Urban art can be a creative way in which to talk about important topics. Artur Bordalo, or Bordalo II, incorporates rubbish into colourful artworks to raise awareness of ecological issues and sustainability. He has created a series of 3D animals that relate to the impact of consumerism: a giant raccoon near the Centro Cultural de Belém is made of old tyres, spare car parts and home appliances, while a sculptural bee in LX Factory has old fans for eyes and miscellaneous junk for legs.

Like junk, urban art is often disposed of. "When you work in a public space, everything is ephemeral," says Vhils. "Nothing lasts forever, like us." But like the city, which is constantly evolving, new pieces will appear in their place. Lisbon is an ever-changing and receptive open-air museum and what was originally seen as a form of visual pollution, something to be kept underground, is now regarded as an asset to be displayed front and centre on the city's streets. — (M)

Where to find it

01 Doca do Jardim do Tabaco, Alfama
Vhils meets PixelPancho.
02 Rua de São Bento, São Bento
AkaCorleone's pop of colour.
03 Travessa dos Brunos, Prazeres
A horse on the edge of a cliff by US duo Cyrcle.

ABOUT THE WRITER: As editor of this guide, Chloë Ashby spent busy weeks exploring every inch of the sunny Portuguese capital. She enjoyed speaking to three of the city's great urban artists and expanding the parameters of her taste in art.

ESSAY 06

Fresh start
Portugal's self-rediscovery

Portugal was hit particularly hard by the global financial crisis but today, in everything from agriculture to economy, it's flourishing.

by Pedro Santos Guerreiro, editor in chief of 'Expresso'

Thriving businesses

01 Maat, Belém
A museum at the forefront of the cultural revolution in Lisbon.
02 Memmo Hotels, citywide
A hotel group that has recognised the city's potential.
03 José Avillez's restaurants
The Portuguese chef owns and runs several successful Lisbon hotspots.

If you want to hear an empty catchphrase about how a country can bounce back from a crisis, ask a consultant. But if you want to see a country that is doing exactly that, come to Portugal. The statistics may still suggest a fairly indebted economy facing austerity measures but look beyond the financial reports and you'll discover a thriving business environment led by innovation. Portugal hasn't found oil: it has found itself.

One of the keys to the country's turnaround has been its renewed enthusiasm for trade. Exports soared from 31.5 per cent of GDP in 2010 to 44 per cent in 2016. This change came not by being different but by acting differently.

Entrepreneurs have founded small and medium-sized businesses in agriculture, a sector that has seen exports grow at a rate of 3 to 5 per cent a year. Portuguese companies ship natural cork, tomato pulp, wine and olive oil to the rest of the world. And look again: all these products benefit from being, well, Portuguese.

But while agriculture has bounced back, Portugal's economy is also moving in another direction: towards technology. Many of the country's start-ups were present at Web Summit, Europe's biggest technology marketplace, which brought 50,000 entrepreneurs and investors to Lisbon in 2016. Portugal is finally coming good on the promise established with its marketing campaign in 2007, that the country is "The West Coast of Europe": a hi-tech economy boasting sunshine, surf and great

"Look beyond the financial reports and you'll discover a thriving business environment"

quality of life. Paddy Cosgrave, the Irish founder of the event, declared at the end: "I love Lisbon!" And Lisbon loves him. Web Summit has boosted the capital's stature as a great city to invest in.

What Web Summit shows is that this nation's business environment is led by a new cosmopolitan generation that grew up after the 1974 Carnation Revolution. In the 1970s Portugal was a poor country, with one person out of every four illiterate. That rate has dropped to 5 per cent. One third of young Portuguese have a degree and, in low-age education, Portugal ranks above countries such as the US, France and Sweden. Investment in education has been the bedrock for our success today.

As political analyst Nicolau Pais puts it, "Portuguese resilience stems from its internal history, written in many pages of poverty and the country's eagerness to fight back." It's a country that has learnt the hard way the meaning of "austerity" but now it is teaching itself a new word: "audacity". By emerging stronger, by innovating and using its natural resources – including its history – it is making itself ready to sail into the future. And that's why change came from within. — (M)

ABOUT THE WRITER: Pedro Santos Guerreiro is based in Lisbon and has been the editor in chief of Portuguese weekly *Expresso* since 2014.

ESSAY 07
Nightlife Midas
A new patron saint

——

Since the 1980s the elusive Manuel Reis has been transforming Lisbon into a more cosmopolitan affair – and one of his many clubs, Lux Frágil, into a city institution. One party person pays tribute.

by Joana Stichini Vilela, writer

I remember the first time my mother let me go clubbing. I was 15, it was a friend's sweet-sixteen party – but the bouncer wouldn't let me in. I was more frustrated than sad; at that age, going on a night out is more about achieving a certain status than having fun. Only later in life does a club become the stage on which all cats can be whatever they wish.

For me it happened when I traded Cascais's superficial nightlife for Lisbon's diversity: first the small bars of Bica and Bairro Alto, then the dive bars of Cais do Sodré. And, finally, Lux Frágil.

Like many of the city's institutions, you don't question Lux (as everybody calls it). At least, I didn't. I knew that the music was good, the parties were awesome and sometimes it was difficult to get in. This riverside warehouse was for me the best nightclub in Lisbon.

I didn't consider the fact that it could vanish one day, or that there was a time when it wasn't around. Nor did I consider that somebody had created it – and continues to recreate it year after year with more and more surprising mise-en-scènes, from vintage lighting to life-size polar bears. That somebody, I know now, is Manuel Reis, who has been busy creating and inspiring some of the city's best clubs, shops and restaurants for nearly 40 years. He is also a man paradoxically famous for having never granted an interview.

Undaunted, in 2016 I tried to interview him about his first and most iconic bar, Frágil. I was working on a book about Lisbon in the 1980s and this place had been the epicentre of bohemian Bairro Alto. He was, as he always is, friendly and polite – but he still refused. "After saying no to so many respected journalists over the years there's no way I can talk to anybody now," he said. A few months later he opened yet another nightclub: Rive Rouge, a more discrete affair at Mercado da Ribeira. On the first few nights you could see him strolling around – with black-rimmed glasses and shaven head – making sure that everything went smoothly. It did.

"For years he devoted himself to bringing the latest trends from abroad to peripheral Lisbon"

Unable to question Midas himself, I've asked many people who know him: what's his secret? They are as unanimous in diagnosing his shyness as in proclaiming him a visionary. Some mention his good taste, others his rigour. For years he devoted himself to bringing the latest trends from abroad to peripheral Lisbon. But now that our city is as worldly as any, how do you explain his golden touch? Maybe you can't.

More clubs

01 Casa Independente, Anjos
A leafy terrace perfect for drinking and dining.
02 Musicbox, Cais do Sodré
Indie rock acts and clubbing in cavernous surroundings.
03 Rio Maravilha, Alcântara
Enjoy drinks with a tropical vibe and a river view.

One thing that's easy to account for is Lux's popularity. It's a forward-thinking nightclub that makes you feel alive and shows that a club can be as intertwined with a city as a patron saint. In fact, my memories of it involve one of my favourite things in Lisbon: the cheerful Saint Anthony feasts. One long, hot, summer night, as I entered at five or six in the morning, I even smelt the stench of grilled sardines instead of the notes of cigarettes and perfume. Even by Lisboeta standards, following an evening of kitschy music, barbecued fish and beer with a night of clubbing seems peculiar. But Lux brings together a fraternity of happy revellers who don't discriminate between hitting the most cosmopolitan dance floor in the city and eating sardines with their fingers.

Last year Lux hosted a series of themed matinées, one of which was the 10-year anniversary of a cult radio talkshow. It was the perfect excuse for many of us – now tired parents of small children – to reunite at that industrial warehouse with the river-facing balcony. Not at seven in the morning to watch the sunrise but at seven in the evening to watch the sunset – and keep on dancing afterwards. — (M)

i

ABOUT THE WRITER: Joana Stichini Vilela is a freelance writer and television host. She's the author of a trilogy of books about life in Lisbon in previous decades.

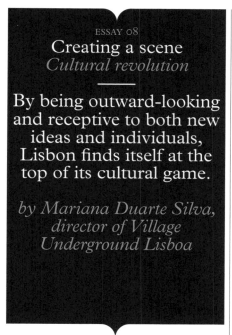

ESSAY 08
Creating a scene
Cultural revolution

___

By being outward-looking and receptive to both new ideas and individuals, Lisbon finds itself at the top of its cultural game.

by Mariana Duarte Silva, director of Village Underground Lisboa

What's happening in Lisbon right now is a cultural revolution. When I was growing up here, very few foreigners visited – and if they did they were simply tourists passing through on their way to either the Algarve or Porto. Lisbon wasn't much of a destination for tourists, let alone creative expats. But suddenly, over the past few years, the city has exploded.

This revolution is down to a boom in artistic and cultural activity in the city. It's thanks to the hard work of Portuguese artists and entrepreneurs, many of whom, like me, grew up as part of Generation X. We're a bunch that looks towards the future: our parents' generation were overshadowed by the dictatorship but we don't want to be defined by its repression and secrecy, nor that of the Catholic Church. We're a generation of innovators and we embrace technology. The rise of millenials has thrown new layers of creativity into the urban mix, embedded in the world of digital marketing, apps and new electronic music. And of course, whatever demographic you happen to fall under, everyone loves a party.

Many of us have spent time working abroad. Portugal's economy has been marked by recessions so lots of people had to leave, while others were simply curious. With few foreigners coming here, we had to get out to see for ourselves what was going on in other parts of the world. Like our adventurous forefathers, we gathered together these global ideas, brought them home and gave them a Portuguese twist.

> *"Like our adventurous forefathers, we gathered together these global ideas, brought them home and gave them a Portuguese twist"*

Today the world is waking up to our city's potential. More and more creative people from other parts of Europe, the Americas and beyond are coming to Lisbon, not only for summer holidays but also to live and work, investing their time and creativity to further improve the city. Of course, this influx has been stimulated by low house prices compared to other capitals, as well as beautiful weather and that certain crumbling charm that the city has. But there is more to it than that: people are also recognising the city's cultural wealth and diversity, which has been richly infused for decades with the music, food and art that has been introduced to Portugal by immigrants from its former colonies.

My own business, Village Underground Lisboa, is the sister project of a cultural platform that was founded in London in 2006. Like the latter, it's a co-working space with a café and events area; we create a flow of artists and co-workers between Lisbon, London and further afield. I witness the benefits that this internationalism brings to projects here, including new international avenues for products, new client bases in Europe and Portugal's former colonies and, of course, new audiences and partnerships for artists.

Village Underground is one of many projects that started abroad and now has a foothold here. Second Home, a creative co-working space that has its headquarters in London's Shoreditch, has opened a new office space above Mercado da

Cultural projects

01 Boom Festival
One of Portugal's largest independent arts and electronic-music festivals.
02 Tremor Festival
Interdisciplinary arts festival on the Azores.
03 Out Jazz
Music plays in parks from May to September.

Ribeira, which is itself a hub for chefs and restaurateurs from around the world. Second Home hosts a plethora of international organisations, not just digital nomads avoiding the winter in their chillier homelands but people who are keen to become a part of the fabric of the city.

With the influx of foreigners and outside investment comes a certain fear for the future of Lisbon. The main concerns are property prices and jobs. Rent is steadily on the rise, boosted by the arrival of Airbnb, which caters not only for tourists but also for expats who are accustomed to living in shoeboxes in London, Paris and New York, and are willing to pay extra for housing. Naturally, this is fuelling resentment among certain Lisboetas, who are being squeezed out of the centre. What the city needs to do is ensure that foreigners and locals are able to live and work in tandem.

Some great initiatives are doing just that. The government is issuing grants and developing mentorship programmes to support Portuguese start-ups. Social projects such as A Avó Veio Trabalhar are empowering older people by giving them opportunities to share their skills with the young. Meanwhile, Pão a Pão, Lisbon's first Syrian restaurant, employs only refugees and helps them integrate in society. "Lisbon is extremely inclusive and accepting," says the latter's co-founder, Francisca Gorjão Henriques. "We haven't heard a bad word said about immigrant communities in our work and we're looking forward to running workshops that celebrate not just the cuisine but also the dance, music and other arts from Middle Eastern countries."

I've never been prouder to be Portuguese – and a Lisboeta in particular. Our diverse artistic scene is testimony to our strength, hard work and ambition. The fact that we're successfully welcoming immigrants from around the world with open arms, both learning from them and inviting them to learn from us, shows how progressive a city we are – and bodes well for the future cultural richness of the country. — (M)

ABOUT THE WRITER: Mariana Duarte Silva is director of Village Underground Lisboa, a co-working and events space in a collection of shipping containers and double-decker busses. She is dedicated to promoting Portuguese artists and women in electronic music.

ESSAY 09
Let's get together
Kiosk culture

———

Lisbon's quirky kiosks have been around since the mid-19th century and are partly responsible for the community spirit that we experience in the city today. Our resident Portuguese reports.

by Carlota Rebelo, Monocle

When I decided to pack my bags and bid farewell to the nation that I had called home since birth, I knew there were a few things that I was going to miss: friends and family, a handful of regular haunts and probably more hours of sunshine a year than I actually need. But on the whole, what could Portugal possibly have that I wouldn't be able to find elsewhere? The answer, I've discovered, is plenty.

It takes feeling at home somewhere else to realise where – or what – your home truly is: it's not a nation, a city or a town but simply a way of being. There's something endearing about the way in which a city can encourage us to create little daily rituals that make our lives worth living. And in Lisbon's case, us creatures of habit are suckers for a certain piece of urban architecture: the humble *quiosque* (kiosk).

Portugal's love affair with these small wrought-iron garden pavilions goes back to the late 1860s and rarely has any other

"It takes feeling at home somewhere else to realise where – or what – your home truly is: it's not a nation, a city or a town but simply a way of being"

structure been so representative of a nation's spirit. By the time the first *quiosques* appeared in the city, the trend had already spread across Europe. City hall saw them as a practical means of embellishing the capital and from the start they sported the same Moorish-meets-art nouveau look for which they are still known to this day. Open on at least one side, the *quiosque* was the perfect hybrid between a café and a bar – in a more central location and, most importantly, more affordable.

From the moment they appeared, Lisbon was a changed city. People bubbled with excitement over these new meeting places. In the early hours of the morning you would see blurry-eyed workers lined up along the counters, swallowing shots of *expresso* – or something stronger – to kickstart the day. And while they were mainly hangouts for the working class in the beginning, it didn't take long for a more eccentric and intellectual clientele to become *quiosque* regulars, particularly after dinner when spirited debates would extend into the wee hours. They started off selling solely drinks and nibbles but soon all sorts of goods were on offer too: tobacco and newspapers, as well as lottery and theatre tickets. In the riverfront *quiosques* you could even find fried fish and olives, catering for the personnel working in the docks near Cais do Sodré.

The newfound hustle and bustle of life in Lisbon came to a halt in the late 1930s when prime minister António de Oliveira Salazar brought previously democratic Portugal under authoritarian rule. With his Estado Novo dictatorship, gathering together in public was discouraged and in many cases forbidden for fear of people plotting against the state. As a result, many

quiosques closed down or were abandoned and by 1974, when the country was unshackled from the regime, the culture had all but disappeared. The few that remained, or managed to claw their way back in the late 1980s, were the exception.

It's only recently that Lisbon has gone through a *quiosque* revolution, pioneered by local entrepreneurs. By embracing its past it has propelled itself into the future and today, strolling through the tree-lined squares and gardens, you'll stumble upon restored decades-old structures and new ones that still somehow exude a vintage charm (*see page 109*). Offering everything from quintessential Portuguese treats and drinks to sushi and tapas, they are once again a staple in the cityscape and the epicentre of daily life for Lisboetas.

It took me a while but I now recognise the impact that these little one-man booths have had in defining who we are: *quiosques* are a gateway, conversation-starters that bring the community together and, most likely, the root of why we love to eat and drink alfresco. As for me, I now know what I can only find in Portugal: a day in the sun, in a leafy square, with a cold glass of *amarguinha* (almond liqueur) in one hand and a newspaper in the other. — (M)

Top kiosks

01 **Quiosque do Adamastor, Santa Catarina**
Enjoy stunning river views.
02 **Quiosque Lisboa-Sé, Alfama**
The place to sip *ginjinha*.
03 **Quiosque do Mercado, Estrela e Lapa**
An art nouveau number from the early 1900s.

ABOUT THE WRITER: Carlota Rebelo is a producer for Monocle 24 and our resident Portuguese. Working across various news shows and *The Urbanist*, she has spoken to mayors, planners and urban leaders about what makes a city – like this one – tick.

ESSAY 10
Avian allure
Portugal's swallows

Small but courageous, adventurous and playful, the swallow is a soaring national symbol that was chosen by the people because of its affinity with the Portuguese character.

by Josh Fehnert, Monocle

Laid low, except for the occasional spire, and spread across seven rolling hills, Lisbon is a city of winding lanes, pitched roofs and canary-yellow trams that chunter up and down steep and storied streets. There's so much for the human eye to delight in, it might be tempting to think that we're the only ones here. But peek up at the eaves of the orange-tiled buildings or into the coiled canopies of the purple-blooming jacaranda trees. See the darting shadows cast against the mosaic-like pavements and you'll likely spot another perspective on Lisbon swooping a few storeys above head height: handfuls of fast-moving swallows, their forked tails silhouetted against the cloudless Iberian sky.

Sadly these hardy birds won't lead you to any secret beaches or under-the-radar restaurants (in truth they're more likely to plop an unappetising present into your coffee from above). Yet considering Portugal's beloved migratory swallow for a moment might help visitors understand the massive distance that Lisbon itself has covered over the past few decades: a transformation that's seen the city shift from a troubled backwater to a skint and dilapidated Atlantic outlier – and finally to its current state as one of Europe's most hopeful and entrepreneurial enclaves.

For many decades the only avian mascot heralded here in Portugal was rather less attractive than the chirpy swallow: the Galo de Barcelos (literally "Rooster of Barcelos"). You'll still spot him emblazoned on tourist tat. He's a black-feathered fowl with a proud red wattle and many-hued pointilist flowers and hearts adorning his saddle, tail and wings. The one, if you know it, that the South African-Portuguese chicken chain Nandos also slapped on its chicken-touting shopfronts.

The rooster's highly apocryphal first strut in the national consciousness isn't really important but stems from 17th-century Braga region in northwest Portugal. The rooster's reputation, however, took a questionable turn when the bird underwent a resurgence as a symbol of nationhood and unity under the brutally fascist António de Oliveira Salazar regime (which lasted from 1932 until 1974). By the end of Salazar's tortuous tenure, the nation gravely needed something to be hopeful about, a new mascot to champion without the burdens of the past.

Luckily, affection for another native bird was hatching. Now, nailed to walls, in kitchens and hung above front doors were flocks of ceramic swallows: tiny symbols of hope in a hopeless time, of resilience against overwhelming odds. Lisbon's love affair with the *andorinha* was taking flight. The bird somehow encapsulated something of the nation and its capital. Spirited but small, the swallow – like the Portuguese diaspora, mercantile Lisboetas or colonial sailors of old – migrated great distances before returning home to nest.

Many of the ceramic swallows still seen in Lisbon today were made by an age-old firm called Bordallo Pinheiro. After a few tough years in which it almost

"Look past the burnt-Sienna roofs and uppermost branches of the hackberry trees and scan the sky for a small, arrow-tailed symbol of optimism"

> **Get the swoop**
> ——
> **01 Route finder**
> Swallows stay close to coasts as they migrate.
> **02 Breeds**
> You'll see the blue barn swallow and a rarer red-rumped variety.
> **03 Martins**
> These closely related birds have squared (rather than forked) tails.

closed down, the company was revived in part by the enterprising intervention of journalist-turned-retailer Catarina Portas. Portas's A Vida Portuguesa shops (*see page 49*) – today, there are two in Chiado, a third in Intendente and a fourth in Mercado da Ribeira – championed and sold the mascot as a broader symbol of optimism: of the indomitable spirit that saw Lisbon weather its share of earthquakes, some of them social, political and economic.

How did Lisbon become a glittering light of the Lusophone world and a beacon of good living, good cheer and great quality of life? For one answer look past the burnt-Sienna roofs and uppermost branches of the hackberry trees and scan the sky for a small, arrow-tailed symbol of optimism. To understand Lisbon a little better, stop for a moment and admire the *andorinhas*. — (M)

ABOUT THE WRITER: Josh Fehnert is MONOCLE's food and travel editor and a long-time visitor to and admirer of the Portuguese capital. His top tips? Stroll through Baixa, shop in Chiado and don't bother getting to the airport early: it's blissfully close to town.

ESSAY 11
Fishy business
Sardines as culinary icon

While Lisbon is invaded by swathes of tourists year on year, a small fish holds its ground on menus throughout the city. Resistance is futile.

by Luis Leal Miranda, writer

Lisbon, November 2016. A new shop opens on the city's main square, Rossio. It's big and bright, decorated with a small merry-go-round, a Ferris wheel and other scaled-down carnival rides. The employees are dressed as circus ringmasters because, well, they work in a shop that sells sardines in a can.

The whole thing doesn't seem right but somehow I'm drawn in by the sudden appearance of a sardine Disneyland. I go inside and it gets better. Hundreds of cans line the walls, each of them stamped with a year, from 1916 to 2016, and some trivia. I pick the one that says "1996" and learn from the metal container that Dolly the sheep was born that year. Now here's a great way to celebrate the first cloning of a mammal and have lunch, I thought.

The shop is called O Mundo Fantástico da Sardinha Portuguesa (The Fantastic World of Portuguese Sardines) and is a shameless, yet somewhat sophisticated, tourist trap. There's nothing new to it: canned sardines have been around forever and tourist traps have existed since the fridge magnet was invented. I've seen my fair share of sardine-shaped fridge magnets – but this?

Lisbon has experienced an unprecedented growth in tourism over the past few years. Cruise ships are now part of the landscape, rising from the river like temporary floating mountains, and short-term rentals have turned traditional neighbourhoods into expensive "Airbnbeehives". Meanwhile, we've all learned how to spell "gentrification". The G-word has brought big changes: hotels have sprouted like mushrooms, rental prices have risen like magic beanstalks and public transport has become a source of public outrage.

It took me a while to get used to such changes but I was dealing with it. Until, that is, I entered The Fantastic World of Portuguese Sardines. What did it mean? Was this our sombrero, our Russian doll, the Portuguese version of the "I love NY" T-shirt?

I felt a change, like the city had become self-aware, conscious of its winning qualities and willing to sell out. The thought troubled me but I kept passing by the shop until it began to blend in with the landscape, like living room wallpaper – albeit of an unusually garish variety.

"The G-word has brought big changes: hotels have sprouted like mushrooms, rental prices have risen like magic beanstalks and public transport has become a source of public outrage"

The warm days arrived and the city turned into its sunny self: relaxed, lazy and with that famous light glistening on the cobbled streets, tiled houses and silver-blue river. And with it came the smell. In the last days of spring the atmosphere in Lisbon attains a new layer, the "sardinosphere": a combination of

Tips for eating sardines

01 Olive oil
Don't be shy with it.
02 Use your hands
Pinch the middle with your index finger and thumb to withdraw the meat.
03 If eaten on bread…
…ask the waiter to toast it a little.

grilled fish, carbon monoxide and oxygen that can be especially potent in the historic city centre. Outdoor grilling becomes a national sport as soon as the weather permits. And sardines – fresh sardines – turn into an obsession the minute they get to the fish market.

Where British people talk about the weather year-round, Lisboetas discuss sardines from May to September. "Have you tried them this year? Are they any good?" This is the kind of conversation that gets you through a ride in a lift here.

Every menu features these small fish. One serving of sardines means six of these swimming beauties accompanied by boiled potatoes, a lettuce-and-tomato salad, onions and roasted bell peppers. Olive oil is mandatory, as is vinegar, and you're in charge of the seasoning.

But grilled sardines are demanding – unlike their canned, ready-to-chew cousins. They're bony, small and hard to eat. They require technique. There are little pieces of flesh hidden beneath the skin and careless diners are in danger of accidentally biting through small but lethal fish bones. (If you do, wash them down with a chunk of bread.) Watching the tourists at riverside terraces ordering sardines and struggling to eat them can be a fun (if sadistic) spectator sport.

I spent many years trying to eat them correctly and I'm still not confident in my deboning skills. Once at an *arraial*, a popular summer fair with loud folk music, I was handed a sardine on top of a slice of bread – which is the right way to eat them, according to the orthodox sardinophiles. I was struggling to take the skin off when I noticed an old couple regarding me with disgust. There I was, hungry and alone, trying to eat under the scrutiny of the sardine police. All of a sudden the woman came up to me and said, "Please stop, I can't watch this anymore." She proceeded to strip the meat off of the bones and hand-feed it to me. I thanked her as she withdrew. "Aren't you going to eat the eye?" she asked. "It's the best bit!"

Lisbon has changed. Today there's a canned version of the city: pretty, warm, easy-to-chew, stay-in-a-hostel, join-a-tour-group Lisbon. And then there's the demanding, mysterious, harsh, beautiful and soulful Lisbon. There are no YouTube tutorials for deboning sardines and there's no quick and painless way to be part of the city. It's a tough lover – an acquired taste – but it's worth the effort. You can't buy this kind of experience – especially not in a can. — (M)

ABOUT THE WRITER: Luis Leal Miranda is a writer for *Time Out Lisbon* and editor of the *Time Out Azores* guide. Although he's lived in Lisbon since 2001, he still hasn't mastered the art of eating sardines.

ESSAY 12
Heart's desire
Hooked by 'saudade'

———

'Saudade', the almost untranslatable Portuguese feeling of joyful sadness, can be keenly felt throughout the capital and keep you coming back for more – even if you're not entirely sure what it means.

by Anja Mutic,
writer

The first time I laid eyes on Lisbon I felt a strange kind of wistfulness. It didn't make sense because I had never been to Portugal: there was nothing to be wistful about. En route from the airport to the centre we passed tumbledown façades, a tall palm tree here and there poking out between the abandoned buildings.

On that first visit I stayed in Castelo, an old neighbourhood with crooked streets and gabled houses; I slept at Palácio Belmonte (*see page 22*), a 10-suite hideaway in a 1449 palace that sits atop ancient Roman and Moorish walls. Standouts among my many vivid memories include vistas of once-grand townhouses, laundry-laden balconies and wrinkle-faced ladies gazing pensively out of their windows. I also remember that moment I first stood on the Miradouro de Santa Luzia, a lookout with a view over neighbouring Alfama's rooftops, the river and the dome of the Panteão Nacional, all framed by grapevine-draped lattices.

I've since lost count of my touchdowns at Lisbon Airport, each of which involves a dramatic arrival: it always appears as if the plane is going to land on the terracotta rooftops. On one particular Sunday morning a few years ago I landed as the day was breaking: everything was half-dark, slow and still. Fado played on the radio in my taxi – a fitting welcome. And there it was again, that same wistfulness. I recognised it so distinctly as the car slid through the empty streets.

I now know the name of this wistfulness: it's called *saudade* in Portuguese. Like Denmark's hygge or the Swedish *lagom*, it's a word that eludes translation. Some describe it as melancholy, others a sweet sadness. It's akin to the love that lingers after someone is gone. But it's not just about loss: it can be a yearning or nostalgia. *Saudade* is like a thread that weaves in and out of all aspects of Portuguese

"'Saudade' is like a thread that weaves in and out of all aspects of Portuguese society; it's the foundation of the country's mentality"

society; it's the foundation of the country's mentality, a tune that forever plays subtly in the background. And it's not surprising. A former colonial powerhouse, Portugal had it all before it lost so much of what it was proud of. Its steady decline from a once rich and powerful monarchy, with its golden era during the Age of Discoveries, to a country struck hard by the debt crisis left its mark. No wonder *saudade* has since become omnipresent.

I have a soft spot for nostalgia, the bittersweet remembrance of the past – so, really, it's also no wonder that I love this city. I love walking through the half-empty streets on a quiet afternoon, past yellow funiculars and rickety trams that clamber up and down the cobbled hills. I love listening to bluesy fado seeping out from half-closed bars in Alfama and stumbling across laundry lines zigzagging their way through narrow alleyways. I love strolling through unexpected squares filled with greenery and eating *pastéis de nata* on the waterfront district of Belém. During the 15th century, explorers set out from here to discover the world – this very

same world in which today so little remains to be discovered.

I was hooked by *saudade* so strongly that a couple of years after that initial visit I returned. The idea was to visit friends and spend a summer month by the Rio Tejo, writing up a storm. I found a small apartment on the top floor of a run-down building in Bairro Alto, a quarter known for its languid days and raucous nights. From one side of my living room I could see the Castelo de São Jorge.

I came back to Lisbon the following year, left again and then returned. Over the years I kept coming and going – and I still do. I revisit Lisbon every chance I get, to listen to a little fado, get lost on aimless hillside wanders and take in that enchanted light. Something tells me it's *saudade* that keeps luring me back, triggering my senses in ways so seductive and poignant that I can't resist. — (M)

'Saudade' sweet spots
———
01 Ride a tram
Take Tram 28 from Martim Moniz to Campo de Ourique.
02 Listen to fado
Head to the cosy Tasca do Chico in Bairro Alto.
03 Look out over the Tejo
Sit by Cais do Sodré and soak in the river views.

ABOUT THE WRITER: Anja Mutic is a writer who splits her time between Zagreb, Croatia and New York. Although she calls Lisbon her impossible love, she has had an affair with the city for 15 years and returns frequently.

Culture
—— Flying colours

Museums and galleries
Painting a picture

Lisbon's culture scene is about more than faded azulejos and moody fado. The city may have been late to the party – there was no public museum with a permanent collection of modern or contemporary art until 2006 – but it certainly made an entrance. And, on the subject of parties, Lisbon has enough late-night venues to satisfy the most ardently nocturnal.

Over the past few years a handful of internationally minded museums have emerged. Today they cover everything from ancient art to cutting-edge technology and often have beautiful gardens to boot. New commercial galleries are also sprouting across the city and range from industrial affairs to flashy white-box spaces.

Add vibrant cultural centres, old and new theatres and art-house cinemas and you have a dynamic line-up befitting a European cultural capital. Lisbon is a receptive city and with more public funding for the arts, as well as a growing number of visiting dealers and collectors, it's having a cultural moment. The trick is not to lose momentum.

① Museu Nacional do Azulejo, São João
On the tiles

This bright and airy museum, a short taxi ride from the city centre, charts the development of Portuguese tiles from the 16th century to the present day.

The building – a former convent from 1509 – is as beautiful as the azulejos within. On the ground floor is the baroque *igreja* (church), a riot of colour with vibrant paintings of saints and blue-and-white tiles displaying bucolic pastoral scenes. And don't miss the glass-roofed cloister, surrounded by two tiers of columns and arches.
4 Rua da Madre de Deus, 1900-312
+351 21 810 0340
museudoazulejo.pt

2
Maat, Belém
Culture shock

Opened in 2016, the riverside Maat (Museu de Arte, Arquitetura e Tecnologia) is funded by the cultural arm of the country's largest energy company, Energias de Portugal (EDP). The museum has changed the city's cultural landscape – and not only because it's spread across a handsome 20th-century red-brick power station and a cutting-edge structure clad in ceramic tiles (*see page 112*).

Maat presents rotating displays of EDP's collection of more than 250 Portuguese artists, as well as national and international exhibitions that marry art, architecture and technology. The new building is divided into four discrete galleries that host site-specific works, video art and sound installations. In the renovated power station, which was operated by the foundation until 1975, a permanent exhibition tells the story of the building as well as the evolution of electricity. Come here to walk among the multicoloured snaking pipes and historic machinery (just keep a wary eye out for the eerily lifelike mannequins).
Avenida Brasilia, 1300-598
+351 21 002 8130
maat.pt

③

Museu Calouste Gulbenkian,
Avenidas Novas
It takes two

"One museum, two collections."
That's the direction in which UK
director Penelope Curtis is taking
the Museu Calouste Gulbenkian.
Until now the museum's two arms
have functioned as separately
as they appear physically: the
Founder's Collection opened at
one end of the flower-filled garden
in 1969; the Modern Collection
at the other end in 1983.

The Founder's Collection was
accumulated by Armenian oil
magnate Calouste Gulbenkian, who
was advised by Howard Carter:
the man who discovered the tomb
of Tutankhamun. It contains
some 6,000 pieces that stretch
from 2600BC to the 20th century,
from colourful mosque lamps and
Iznik pottery to French furniture
and illuminated manuscripts.
The continually growing Modern
Collection, which has been pieced
together by the foundation, tells
the story of Portuguese art in the
20th century. It's also continually
rotating: out of the 11,000 works
in the collection, 500 are on display
at any given time.

A series of "Conversations"
sees works shift between the two
collections. The result? A melange
of objects that blur geographical
and temporal boundaries. The
two buildings also boast five
auditoriums between them, one of
which is outdoors. Oh, and there's
a lovely lake in the public garden.
*45A Avenida de Berna, 1067-001
+ 351 21 782 3461
gulbenkian.pt*

④
Mude, Baixa
In fine style

The centrally located Museu do
Design e da Moda, known as Mude
(Portuguese for "change"), is at the
forefront of the cultural revolution
in Lisbon. Having opened in the
Centro Cultural de Belém (*see page
102*) in 1999, it closed in 2006
and reopened again in its current
pared-back space – the cavernous
former HQ of the Banco Nacional
Ultramarino – in 2009.

The third floor hosts the
permanent collection donated by
private collector Francisco Capelo,
while the open-plan second, fourth
and fifth floors – as well as the
underground vault, which still
contains safe-deposit boxes – are
dedicated to temporary exhibitions
and events. The overarching aim?
To explore the links between
fashion and design, as well as their
relationship with technology, the
environment and the economy.
*24 Rua Augusta, 1100-053
+ 351 21 817 1892
mude.pt*

⑤
Museu Coleção Berardo, Belém
Modern marvel

This modern and contemporary-
art museum opened in the Centro
Cultural de Belém (*see page 102*)
in 2007 and invites visitors to
mosey through the main artistic
movements of the 20th century.

The majority of the permanent
collection, which is found on the
first and second floors, comes
from Madeira-born art collector
Joe Berardo. The second floor is
dedicated to works created between
1900 and 1960, from cubism to
pop art; highlights include Dalí's
painted-wood lobster perched on a
bakelite telephone and Yves Klein's
seductive bright-blue female torso.
The more open-plan first floor
continues from 1960 to 1990.
Meanwhile, temporary exhibitions
keep things as fresh as the tranquil
garden, which is complete with
water features and a reclining
figure by Henry Moore.
*Praça do Império, 1449-003
+ 351 21 361 2878
museuberardo.pt*

One-man band

The Museu Rafael Bordalo
Pinheiro in Campo Grande
was the first museum in
Portugal to be purpose-built
to house an artist's collection.
Opened in 1916, it features
everything from paintings to
ceramics and caricatures.
*museubordalopinheiro.
cm-lisboa.pt*

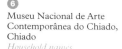

Museu Nacional de Arte
Contemporânea do Chiado,
Chiado
Household names

Home to a collection of Portuguese
art from 1850 to the present, as
well as some French sculptures
from the late 1800s, the Museu
Nacional de Arte Contemporânea
do Chiado (MNAC) is where you
come to see the big national names.

Since it was founded in 1911,
the MNAC has been housed in the
former convent of São Francisco
da Cidade – which was badly
damaged by a fire in 1988 and
reopened in 1994. The ash-grey
interior is all stone, metal, wood
and glass, with a high-ceilinged
atrium and suspended walkway.
The barrel-vaulted Gabinete
de Desenhos (Drawing Room)
is reminiscent of the building's
monastic origins, while the terrace
is the perfect spot to sit in the sun
with a coffee and a Rodin.
4 Rua Serpa Pinto, 1200-444
+351 21 343 2148
museuartecontemporanea.gov.pt

(7)
Museu Nacional de Arte Antiga,
Santos
Painterly perch

This boxy yellow museum opened
in 1884 and contains paintings,
sculptures, jewellery and decorative
arts from the 12th to the 19th
century. Start on the third floor and
work your way down. At the top
you'll find Portuguese paintings
and sculptures, including Nuno
Gonçalves's group portrait "Panels
of Saint Vincent" (1470). Level
two hosts art from the Portuguese
discoveries (a tad less thrilling) and
the first floor European paintings.
Alternatively, make a beeline for
the sculpture-specked garden.
Rua das Janelas Verdes, 1249-017
+351 21 391 2800
museudearteantiga.pt

⑩
Museu Nacional dos Coches, Belém
Wealth on wheels

Set back from the ships on the Rio Tejo, you'll find another, slightly less buoyant, fleet: a collection of 17th, 18th and 19th-century carriages and coaches from France, Spain, Portugal and beyond.

Originally (and still partly) housed in Palácio de Belém's 18th-century riding school on Praça Afonso de Albuquerque, in 2015 most of the collection moved to a new building by Brazilian architect Paulo Mendes da Rocha. The latter concrete setting is striking but lacking in historical reference – and therein lies some controversy.
*136 Avenida da Índia, 1300-300
+351 21 073 2319
museudoscoches.pt*

⑧
Atelier-Museu Júlio Pomar,
São Bento
Going solo

When Portuguese artist Júlio Pomar decided to create a museum dedicated to himself, he knew who to turn to: architect Álvaro Siza Vieira oversaw the redesign of this 17th-century former warehouse, converting it into a sleek exhibition space spread across two floors.

Opened in 2013, the atelier-museum displays more than 400 works by one of the greatest names in contemporary Portuguese art. It also features a library, where you can flick through printed intrigues and newspaper cutouts that both explain and elevate the impact of Pomar's work.
*7 Rua do Vale, 1200-472
+351 21 588 0793
ateliermuseujuliopomar.pt*

⑨
Casa-Museu Medeiros e Almeida,
Liberdade e Castilho
House proud

Despite being located in the city centre, the Casa-Museu Medeiros e Almeida is a quieter choice when it comes to museums. The decorative arts collection of Portuguese businessman António de Medeiros e Almeida is displayed across 26 galleries in his former home, which was extended in 1968 and converted into a private museum in 1973. As you stroll through the rooms take note of the difference between the old and new wings: the former was lived in whereas the latter, which is more lavish, was kitted out specially for the museum.

The 2,000-piece collection includes everything from pocket watches to paintings and dates from the 2nd to the 20th century. Highlights include a Chinese porcelain bidet that belonged to the French royal family.
*41 Rua Rosa Araújo, 1250-194
+351 21 354 7892
casa-museumedeirosealmeida.pt*

⑪
Museu do Oriente, Alcântara
Look east
There's nothing fishy about this museum – except that it's housed in a revamped preserved-cod warehouse. It's a little out of the way, plonked between a main road and the river, but worth a visit. Inside the big concrete building, which is adorned with gold leaf, is a story of east-west exchange.

The permanent collection on the first floor is about the Portuguese presence in Asia: don't miss the rosewood equestrian statue from Timor-Leste. The second floor is devoted to the colourful Chinese Opera and its stylised characters.
*Avenida Brasília, Doca de Alcântara (Norte), 1350-352
+351 21 358 5200
museudooriente.pt*

Galeria Madragoa, Santos
Small wonder

Behind its bright-blue door and traditional blue-and-white azulejo façade, Galeria Madragoa hosts cutting-edge artists from Portugal, Italy, Poland, Mexico and Ecuador. This contemporary-art gallery was co-founded by Matteo Consonni, the Italian former director of Galleria Franco Noero in Turin, and Portuguese biologist Gonçalo Jesus (*both pictured, Jesus on left*). The pair met while studying at London's Goldsmiths and opened this gallery in a former *paderia* (bakery) on a quiet residential street in bohemian Santos in 2016.

Madragoa is a young gallery working with young artists. The street-side space is fast-changing – and small, making for an intimate and approachable feel – and the focus tends to be on solo shows that rotate every six weeks. Adding to the flexibility is a second exhibition space that the pair opened above the main gallery in 2017: there are two rooms with white walls and wooden floors, one of which can host an artist in residence.
45 Rua do Machadinho, 1200-705
+351 21 390 1699
galeriamadragoa.pt

②
Galeria Francisco Fino, Marvila
New kid on the block

From 2012 to 2016, Francisco Fino (*pictured*) was preoccupied with what he calls his "nomad shows", exhibiting artwork across the city. In 2017 he opened his eponymous gallery in a vast 19th-century olive-oil warehouse, which he sensitively refurbished with Lisbon-based GCCM Arquitectos.

An off-centre entrance disrupts the symmetry of the two-storey space and a staircase concealed within a black tube (a sculpture itself) leads to an office. "Like the artwork, the gallery offers different perspectives," says Fino.
76 Rua Capitão Leitão, 1950-052
+351 925 623 717
franciscofino.com

JOSÉ LOUREIRO
Boné
18 ABR → 11 MAIO

❸
Cristina Guerra Contemporary
Art, Estrela e Lapa
Follow the leader

Cristina Guerra (*pictured*), who
founded her eponymous gallery in
2001, is one of the few women to
make a successful career in a still
male-dominated field. Her mission?
To promote Portuguese artists
both at home and abroad and, in
turn, to bring the best international
artists to Lisbon.

The gallery represents more
than 25 emerging and established
artists, from Portuguese painter
and multimedia artist Julião
Sarmento to US conceptual artist
Lawrence Weiner. Across its split-
level space it hosts about six solo
shows a year, as well as occasional
group shows overseen by guest
curators. It also flies the Portuguese
flag at the world's leading
contemporary-art fairs, including
Art Basel and Art Forum Berlin.
*33 Rua de Santo António à Estrela,
1350-291*
+351 21 395 9559
cristinaguerra.com

④
Galeria 111, Campo Grande
Family affair

Opened in 1964 by Manuel de
Brito, who started out selling books
to students at the nearby university,
Galeria 111 is now run by his son
Rui. "Of course it's a business but
it's also a passion," says the latter,
whose mother (*both pictured*) helps
with curating.

Galeria 111 is much more than
a gallery. As well as two spaces
for exhibiting works by both
Portuguese and international artists
– past shows have included those
by António Dacosta and Sonia
Delaunay – there's a jam-packed
archive of artists' catalogues
and letters. There's also a small
bookshop, a framing workshop and
a warehouse-like space piled high
with the family's private collection.
Plus there's the Centro de Arte
Manuel de Brito in the west of
the city, the family's contemporary-
art museum.
113 Campo Grande, 1700-089
+351 21 797 7418
111.pt

❺
Caroline Pagès Gallery, Campo
de Ourique
Home is where the art is

"I didn't want it to be just another
white cube," says French gallerist
Caroline Pagès (*pictured*) of her
gallery, which opened on the first
floor of a 1925 apartment building
in 2007. With seven small rooms,
complete with wooden floors
and stucco ceilings, it still has a
residential feel. She sees the layout
as a challenge: "The exhibition
has to unfold piece by piece." The
gallery represents Portuguese,
North African and French artists,
with a room for residencies.
*12 Rua Tenente Ferreira Durão,
1350-315*
+351 21 387 3376
carolinepages.com

Old guard

Galeria Pedro Cera in
Campo de Ourique has been
a key player on the city's
commercial-gallery scene since
1998. It represents both local
and international artists in its
white-walled gallery, which was
expanded in 2008 to include
two exhibition spaces.
pedrocera.com

⑥
Galeria 3 + 1, São Bento
Grow with the flow

James Steele (*pictured*) moved to
Lisbon in 2010, having worked for
galleries in London and Madrid.
"I'm from Sydney originally
and I basically missed having a
beach," he says. It was here that
he joined co-director Jorge Viegas
at Galeria 3 + 1, which represents
contemporary artists from Portugal
and further afield.

In 2017, just in time for its 10th
anniversary, the ever-growing
gallery moved from Chiado to
a former printing house in São
Bento; the two-storey space offers
artists better visibility.
2 Largo Hintze Ribeiro, 1250-122
+351 21 017 0765
3m1arte.com

Underdogs

A commercial gallery that
hosts about six exhibitions a
year, a public-art programme
that promotes urban art and
a shop that sells original and
affordable artist editions:
Underdogs is a multifaceted
cultural platform.

It was founded in 2010 by
Portuguese artist Alexandre
Farto, commonly known as
Vhils; the son of an accountant
and maths teacher, he briefly
studied at Central Saint
Martins in London and shot
to fame when he carved a
portrait on a wall with Banksy.
Today he oversees the three
branches of the business with
co-director Pauline Foessel.

The Underdogs Gallery
opened in a former wine
warehouse in Marvila in 2013,
with the aim of bringing young
artists – underdogs – off the
streets and into the gallery.
But they're far from confined
to a white-walled interior: as
well as inviting artists to exhibit
here, Underdogs works with
the Galeria de Arte Urbana,
a department created by city
hall, to facilitate the painting
(and more) of façades across
the city.

The Underdogs Store
opened in 2014 and two years
later moved to a shared space
on the banks of the Rio Tejo.
under-dogs.net

'Yes, I'm the Fernando
Pessoa statue. You're going
to pose with me? Great.'

Cultural centres
All together now

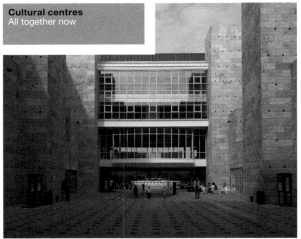

①
Centro Cultural de Belém, Belém
Centre stage

Built to host Portugal's presidency of the EU in 1992, today the Centro Cultural de Belém (CCB) is the most renowned cultural centre in the country. Architects Vittorio Gregotti and Manuel Salgado wanted to create an open-air city where buildings, streets, squares and bridges intertwine. The result is an ode to culture, hosting operas, ballets, touring symphonies and international conferences in myriad rooms, including Lisbon's largest auditorium. Take a trip to the first-floor terrace, where you'll find gardens overlooking the Rio Tejo.
Praça do Império, 1449-003
+ 351 21 361 2400
ccb.pt

Cultural exchange
———
O Apartamento doubles variously as a gallery, pop-up shop, atelier and dining space. It has welcomed visitors from all over the world and hosted a number of events, from a series of concerts by Brazilian musician Cicero to a dinner held by chef Nuno Mendes.
oapartamento.com

②
Fábrica Braço de Prata, Marvila
Open arms

Founded in 2007 by white-bearded philosophy professor Nuno Nabais, after closing his secondhand bookshop in Bairro Alto, Fábrica Braço de Prata is a spot like few others. Spread across three floors of a restored arms factory in Marvila you'll see concert halls, exhibition spaces, screening rooms and conference areas, as well as a bookshop (naturally), a restaurant and a high-ceilinged bar that resembles a living room.

The somewhat ramshackle building is open from 18.00 to 02.00 (04.00 at weekends). It's an ever-evolving creature so you never know what you might encounter unless you check the listings: a jazz quartet in one room, a film screening in another. Plus, as soon as the sun's shining, guests spill out into the graffiti-clad courtyard.
1 Rua da Fábrica de Material de Guerra, 1950-128
+ 351 965 518 068
bracodeprata.com

❸
Culturgest, Roma e Areeiro
Eclectic offering

A stalwart presence at Lisbon's
many film festivals, a growing
reference for the European
experimental theatre circuit,
a stop-off point for visiting
lecturers (or new circus acts) and
a canvas for various showcases
of its 1,700-strong collection of
Portuguese art, this imposing
arts foundation – part of (and
owned by) the Caixa Geral de
Depósitos Foundation – is an
unexpected host for the city's
more avant garde offerings.

The slatted concrete-curve
frontage makes for an impressive
entrance and inside you'll find
two auditoriums, two galleries and
myriad meeting rooms. Just keep
your wits about you: it's easy to
get lost among the volumes of red-
carpeted corridors.
50 Rua Arco do Cego, 1000-300
+351 21 790 5155
culturgest.pt

Fado

The narrow streets of Mouraria
still echo to the doleful sounds
of Portugal's traditional fado.
Its roots can be traced back to
the neighbourhood in the early
1830s, where it was sung in
tavernas, cafés, gardens and
squares. With themes of loss
and sadness, it's a melancholic
genre in which the singer's
powerful voice contrasts with
the 12 steel strings of the
intricate Portuguese guitar.
In the 1870s it was propelled
to stardom after it started
appearing in *teatro de revista*,
a particular form of musical
theatre from Lisbon.

Maria Severa expanded
fado beyond Mouraria's
cobbled streets: her story as
a prostitute-turned-singer
became one of Lisbon's most
iconic tales and was turned
into a book called *A Severa*.

Live venues
Party people

(1)
Galeria Zé dos Bois, Bairro Alto
Note worthy

For the past quarter of a century or so, Galeria Zé dos Bois (ZDB) has been rolling out a remarkable roster of concerts, performances and residencies at a frequency that other more commercial venues in the city might balk at.

Despite the size of the building – a 2,500 sq m former palace that includes a 250-capacity gig room, two floors of gallery space and a charming rooftop terrace – this non-profit association is known for its welcoming ambience, killer live shows and a sense of freedom that has helped it gain fans (some of whom are rather famous) from all over the world. As low-key as ZDB is, its eclectic programme – from exhibitions and lectures to concerts and dance performances – punches well above its weight.
59 Rua da Barroca, 1200-049
+ 351 21 343 0205
zedosbois.org

(2)
Teatro Aberto, Campolide
New material

The independent Teatro Aberto (Open Theatre), directed by João Lourenço, has a mainly contemporary repertoire: come here to catch an experimental piece of music or an original play written for the theatre by a budding author.

Founded in 1976 by Grupo 4, the theatre was taken over by O Novo Grupo and moved to a new purpose-built space near Praça de Espanha in 2002. There are two auditoriums: the smaller Sala Vermelha (Red Room) is preferred for talks and conferences, as well as intimate plays and concerts; the 400-seat Sala Azul (Blue Room) features an orchestra pit and stages larger performances. The light-filled foyer also hosts exhibitions and book launches. Plus, for those curious about what goes on when the curtain falls, there are backstage tours.
Rua Armando Cortez, 1050-107
+ 351 21 388 0086
teatroaberto.com

Let's dance

01 Lounge, Bica
Lounge has been providing a (tight) space for daring punk bands, nostalgic house music and extended vinyl sets since it was opened by two German music-lovers in 1999. With an amply stocked bar and friendly staff, it still keeps regulars dancing until closing time.
loungelisboa.com.pt

02 Damas, Graça
Housed in a former industrial bakery, this bar, kitchen and music venue serves a diverse mix of concerts and parties. Its owners (two ladies, as the name implies) regularly hand the programming reins over to musicians, collectives and promoters.
+351 964 964 416

03 Music Box, Cais do Sodré
Escape the rabble of Lisbon's "pink street" in this compact club, which stays open until the early hours four nights a week. It hosts heavyweight club acts and celebrated local bands but the monthly night dedicated to the homegrown Príncipe label is the jewel in its crown.
musicboxlisboa.com

Main event

Lisbon's leading national theatre, the neoclassical-style Teatro Nacional Dona Maria II, opened in 1846 on the north side of Praça Dom Pedro IV in Baixa. The two stages – the larger Sala Garrett and smaller studio stage – host both in-house and guest productions.
tndm.pt

③
São Luiz Teatro Municipal, Chiado
Something for everyone

Perched on a steep hill in the historic neighbourhood of Chiado, São Luiz Teatro Municipal is full of surprises. Alongside the usual stage settings there's the glass-walled Jardim de Inverno (Winter Garden) complete with a fresco by Italian artist Luigi Manini and, since 2013, the Mini Bar Teatro by José Avillez. The latter, a theatrical stop-in that pays homage to the glitz of cinema, offers playful

cocktails and avant garde plates by the prolific chef.

The theatre was built in 1894 and renovated in both 1928 and 2001. There are three stages: alongside the Winter Garden – which hosts music and theatre, as well as dinners and drinks – the downstairs studio theatre is a small but flexible space and the main auditorium seats more than 700.
38 Rua António Maria Cardoso,
1200-027
+351 21 325 7640
teatrosaoluiz.pt

④
Teatro do Bairro, Bairro Alto
Press gang

Teatro do Bairro opened in 2011 in the former printing press of old daily newspaper *Diário Popular*. Designed by Portuguese architect Alberto de Souza Oliveira, the black-box theatre, which can seat 100, recalls a rehearsing studio.

As well as hosting three or four of its own productions each year, Teatro do Bairro hosts external theatre and dance companies. It's also much more than a theatre, with a bar, stand-up comedy, live music (DJs play until 02.00 on Fridays and Saturdays) and Sunday afternoon film screenings.
63 Rua Luz Soriano, 1200-246
+351 21 347 3358

①
Cinema Ideal, Bairro Alto
Super sequel

When it was originally built in 1908 this intimate space was Lisbon's first fully functioning cinema. It went through many incarnations, including a somewhat risqué period as a theatre for adult films, before closing down in 2013.

After being lovingly restored by Lisbon film aficionado Pedro Borges, it reopened as a beautiful independent cinema in 2014. Sit back in a comfy chair (the same as those used at the Finnish National Opera House) and catch a recent release from Italy or France or an art-house flick.
15-17 Rua do Loreto, 1200-241
+351 21 099 8295
cinemaideal.pt

Cinema São Jorge,
Liberdade e Castilho
Scene-setter

This 1950s gem is one of the city's few remaining old-school cinemas. In a privileged location on the Avenida da Liberdade, it's a beacon of the glory days of the silver screen – and today it's also the prime setting for film festivals.

The former auditorium, which boasted more than 1,800 seats, has now been divided into three smaller rooms. Nonetheless its grandeur endures, with a wood-panelled interior, retro decor and a magnificent balcony adjoined to the upstairs bar and restaurant.

175 Avenida da Liberdade, 1250-141
+351 21 310 3402
cinemasaojorge.pt

③
Cinemateca Portuguesa,
Liberdade e Castilho
All the classics

Founded in the early 1950s by cinema enthusiast Manuel Félix Ribeiro as a museum dedicated to the art of film, today the Cinemateca Portuguesa stands as a proud testament to Portugal's cinematic past.

In a well-preserved late 19th-century building on the elegant Rua Barata Salgueiro you'll find a museum, an archive, a bookshop, a restaurant and, of course, a cinema. It boasts a collection of more than 70,000 cinematographic objets d'art, films and recordings – both in analogue and digital – and about 21,000 of those are the products of Portuguese cinema. Visit for regular screenings, presentations, themed film festivals and more besides.

39 Rua Barata Salgueiro, 1269-059
+351 21 359 6200
cinemateca.pt

Lisbon on film

01 Les Amants du Tage, 1955: This French drama directed by Henri Verneuil takes Lisbon as a backdrop and follows the story of a war veteran turned taxi driver and a woman with a police inspector on her tail. Fado singer Amália Rodrigues graces the soundtrack.

02 Lisbon Story, 1994: The Palácio Belmonte (*see page 22*) takes centre stage in this Wim Wenders masterpiece, which looks at the nature of cinema as a craft. Two cameos to note: Portuguese folk group Madredeus and director Manoel de Oliveira.

03 Sostiene Pereira, 1995: Italian director Roberto Faenza's film is set during the Estado Novo dictatorship and follows journalist Pereira (Marcello Mastroianni), who discovers the true colours of the regime when faced with censorship. Look out for the landmarks.

04 Night Train to Lisbon, 2013: In Bille August's drama we follow Raimund Gregorius (Jeremy Irons) as he embarks on a train journey from Bern to Lisbon in search of a woman he saved from jumping to her death.

Fado was born on a day when the wind barely stirred and the sea elongated the sky…

Media round-up
Word on the streets

❶
Media
Reading material

For the literary sort, ❶ *Ler* magazine has been published every three months since 1987 and showcases stellar writing, from in-depth essays to interviews with top authors. ❷ *Roof* sits at the intersection of design, urbanism and architecture with pleasing results. Plus, if you fancy a fresh approach to interior design, ❸ *Attitude* magazine presents it beautifully – and with a varied texture, due to the use of different paper stocks in each issue.

For a nation only unshackled from dictatorship in the mid-1970s, Portugal's printed news is powerful. Weekly newspaper ❹ *Expresso* digests the week for readers, while design-savvy daily ❺ *i* blends local news with affairs. Based by Lisbon's riverfront, ❻ *Público* often casts an eye beyond the border. For a morning update on the financial markets, ❼ *Jornal de Negócios* has you covered.

Portuguese-language radio

01 Antena 1: The best radio station for news and sport (mainly football) updates. Tune in during the afternoon to discover emerging Portuguese-language performers.
rtp.pt/antena1

02 TSF: Broadcasting from Lisbon since 1989, TSF is a staple for affairs and diplomacy across the nation. As well as hourly bulletins it features shows on global issues.
tsf.pt

03 Rádio Comercial: The latest pop and rock hits from Portugal and beyond. The morning banter is worth listening to: the hosts often create parody songs that riff on the politics of the day.
radiocomercial.pt

Design and architecture
—— Best of the built environment

Rambling hillside alleys, tree-lined squares, breezy *miradouros* gazing out over terracotta roofs: Lisbon's cityscape is so intoxicating that it can distract you from the buildings. That would be a mistake. Between the Parque das Nações in the east and the Mosteiro dos Jerónimos in the west are jaw-dropping structures that span 10 centuries.

Traditional Portuguese architecture is a story of extremes: the opulent Manueline style was followed by the stripped-back, earthquake-resistant Pombaline. This eclecticism continued in the 20th century, with art deco, modernist, brutalist and postmodernist masterpieces dotting the centre. Contemporary architects have forsaken identikit glass skyscrapers in favour of diversity, from the Universidade Nova's rectilinear block to the curvaceous Maat.

The common thread is interaction with the city's natural qualities: the hills, the Rio Tejo and the azure skies that inspired the title "City of Light". Here are our richest discoveries.

①
Azulejos
Miles of tiles

Pretty much everywhere you turn across the city you'll encounter the ubiquitous azulejo, Portugal's decorative ceramic tile. From humble houses to palaces and churches, exquisitely colourful and intricate tilework adorns many of the city's buildings today. However, the azulejo tradition can be traced back as far as 711, when the Moors occupied Lisbon and other parts of Portugal. Hence the name, which is derived from the ancient Arabic word *az-zulayj*, meaning "small polished stone".

Styles and motifs range from religious to rococo, historical to art deco. And examples can be found both inside and out; note the modernist examples lining the walls of Lisbon's metro stations. Many of these were designed by Maria Keil between 1957 and 1982, her work playing a significant role in reviving the azulejo as an art form.

❷
Kiosks
Take a break

Shopping can be unforgiving work. Between heaving all those bags and scaling the city's hills you'll need to take a load off now and again. For a caffeine hit, do as the Lisboetas do and grab a *bica* (espresso) from one of the city's numerous open-air *quiosques* (kiosks). These little one-man establishments are easy to spot: they're made out of forged iron and glass, open on at least one side and traditionally dark green – although you may see the occasional one in red or yellow as well. Selling everything from ice-cold beers to small snacks and other refreshments, *quiosques* are a key part of daily life in Lisbon (*see page 85*).

109

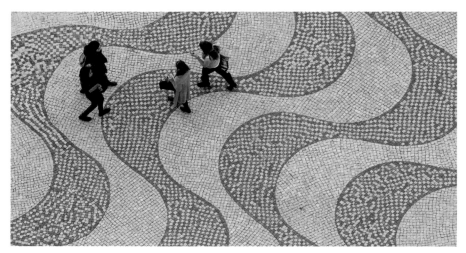

③
Calçada
Set in stone

One of Lisbon's most powerful branding tools is unusually downtrodden: the humble paving stone. The *calçada portuguesa* (Portuguese pavement) forms intricate designs and can be found decorating many of the city's squares, pavements and gardens.

The traditional geometric and figurative patterns are achieved by cutting and shaping each limestone and black-basalt stone by hand and then fitting them into a mould. The paving isn't exclusive to Lisbon, though. Examples can be found wherever Portugal has left its footprint, from Luanda to Rio de Janeiro, Maputo to Macau.

④
Trams
Eléctrico avenues

Picture-perfect views greet the visitor around every corner in Lisbon but no image would be complete without an *eléctrico* (tram) crisscrossing into view. Easy to recognise in their canary-yellow livery, they have been operating in Lisbon since 1901 and in their 1950s heyday there were more than 400 roaming across the capital.

A few of the first carriages were imported from Philadelphia and Saint Louis in the US and most of these still contain their original wood panelling. If you want to travel around the city centre like a local, only the bright-yellow ones are the real deal.

⑤
Street lamps
Lighten up

These intricate lighting fixtures are quiet inhabitants of Lisbon's streets. Made of cast-iron, most were introduced during the Pombaline period in the late 18th century and are traditionally found attached to walls. The more modern versions tend to perch on the end of a post.

As gas lamps were replaced with electric versions, the city made a good job of adapting older models. If you find yourself walking through the cobbled streets of Baixa or Alfama, look closely as many sport Lisbon's coat of arms: a caravel (a small Portuguese ship from the 15th to 17th centuries) flanked by ravens.

Contemporary
Pioneering projects

1

Fundação Champalimaud, Belém
New frontier

The Champalimaud Centre for
the Unknown – a foundation
and facility for advanced medical
research and treatment – was
the vision of the eponymous late
financier António de Sommer
Champalimaud. Completed in
2010, it was one of Indian architect
Charles Correa's final projects and
exhibits his characteristic subtlety
of form. Two units – one private,
the other with a public exhibition
space and auditorium – are linked
by a tubular bridge and arranged
around an outdoor amphitheatre.
Abundant windows and terraces
connect the stark building with the
river and surrounding gardens.

The centre is on the site
where Infante Dom Henrique and
Vasco da Gama departed on their
journeys; for Correa this formed "a
perfect metaphor for the discoveries
of contemporary science today".
Avenida Brasília, 1400-038
+ 351 21 048 0200
fchampalimaud.org

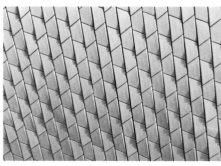

② Maat, Belém
Show white

Many of Lisbon's most prominent contemporary buildings aim to reaffirm the city's relationship with the Rio Tejo but none do it so spectacularly as Amanda Levete's Maat (Museu de Arte, Arquitetura e Tecnologia). A sinuous form that's been grafted onto a 1908 red-brick power station, the appearance of its 15,000 tessellating white tiles shifts with the light. Within, a cave-like central chamber provides low-lit respite from the dazzling riverbank; above, an undulating roof terrace affords panoramic views of Belém and beyond.

Funded by the EDP Foundation, the philanthropic arm of Energias de Portugal (EDP), Maat has become a fixture of the city's arts scene (*see page 94*). Its pre-opening party in 2016 attracted 80,000 visitors, roughly a sixth of Lisbon's urban population at the time.
Avenida Brasília, 1300-598
+351 21 002 8130
maat.pt

③
Reitoria da Universidade Nova de Lisboa, Campolide
Windows on the city

Nova is one of Portugal's most renowned universities, particularly for its business, economics and finance courses. The main campus on the Campolide hill is crowned by the *reitoria* (rectory), completed in 1998 and awarded the 2002 Valmor prize (*see page 122*). It made the name of Lisbon practice Aires Mateus, since responsible for a raft of major buildings in the capital.

A rectilinear construction in glass and stone, the rectory's west-facing side is remarkable for its irregular fenestration, a swarm of narrow slits that controls the natural light. The entrance alcoves are embedded in a vast staircase, which runs across rather than towards the façade. Views from the top to the Parque Florestal de Monsanto echo the scenic *miradouros* that punctuate the cityscape.
Campus de Campolide, 1099-085
+351 21 371 5600
unl.pt

④
Stone Block, Avenidas Novas
Mutant living

Avenidas Novas's orderly early 20th-century grid form contrasts with its architectural sweep and chaotic traffic. Alberto de Souza Oliveira's 2011 Stone Block restores some serenity. The exterior is clad with slim panels of grey-veined marble, shielding 20 apartments from the streets. As residents turn their panels to adjust the light inside, the building's exterior also morphs, so passers-by seldom see the same set-up twice – an effect Oliveira dubbed a "mutant façade".
67 Avenida Defensores de Chaves,
1000-207
lisbonstoneblock.com

⑥
GS1 HQ, Lumiar
Sculpted concrete

One of Lisbon's most idiosyncratic contemporary structures sits in its northern peripheries. The Portuguese base of GS1 was once a drab 1980s office building but a refurbishment by Pedro Appleton of Promontório Architects between 2014 and 2016 changed the structure so drastically as to make it new.

Inside, Appleton designed a sumptuous office furnished with abundant textiles and cork furniture. But the main draw is the trio of façades, each of which displays a diagonally aligned row of concrete bas-reliefs by street artist Vhils. When viewed together, they present a continuous flow of human features, geological formations and visualisations of data, alluding to GS1's role as the creator of QR codes and barcodes.
Estrada do Paço do Lumiar, Campus do Lumiar, Edifício K3, 1649-038
+ 351 21 752 0740
gs1pt.org

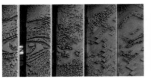

⑤
Energias de Portugal HQ,
Cais do Sodré
Future office

In recent years, architectural studio Aires Mateus has left a trail of delicate and diverse projects across its native city. The Energias de Portugal (EDP) headquarters, which opened in 2015, is the most prominent. Comprising two towers linked by sloping bridges, its dramatic profile slots neatly into the surrounding streetscape. The glass towers project a transparent image, while rows of sail-like shafts control light and heat.

Impressively, most of the complex's large spaces – the entrance, a theatre and service areas such as the carpark – are hidden beneath a public courtyard. The majority of the interiors, designed by big names such as Jasper Morrison and Universal Design Studio, are private but no matter: the plaza is the best place to take in the architecture.
12 Avenida 24 de Julho, 1249-300
edp.pt; airesmateus.com

Just stop the tram whenever you smell 'pastéis de nata'

World Expo 1998
Best in show

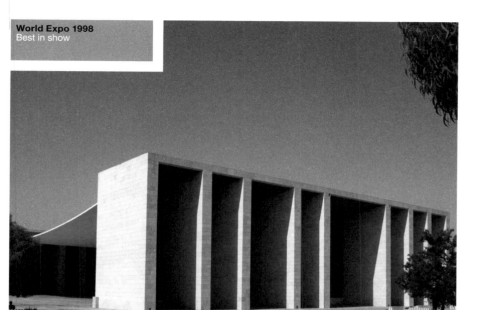

1

Pavilhão de Portugal,
Parque das Nações
Impossible feat

Álvaro Siza Vieira's Portuguese
National Pavilion defies all laws
of physics: at the heart of its design
is an incredibly thin, curvilinear
concrete pall, balancing effortlessly
between two monumental
structures. Inspired by a sheet
of paper balancing on two bricks,
this stunning suspended canopy
provides shade for the immense
public plaza beneath it and creates
a perfectly framed view of the
adjacent Rio Tejo.

Though the pavilion was
the centrepiece of the Parque
das Nações urban-regeneration
programme for the 1998 World
Expo, its interior spaces have
been closed for years, their future
uncertain. It was acquired by the
Universidade de Lisboa in 2015,
so perhaps a practical purpose
will soon become clear. For now,
however, we're more than happy
simply admiring the exterior.
Alameda dos Oceanos, 1990–221

Derelict structures

Several centuries of natural disasters, fires and fluctuating prosperity have left Lisbon with an abundance of dilapidated buildings. The medieval Igreja de São Domingos, for instance, was badly damaged in a 1531 earthquake, nearly levelled in its calamitous 1755 follow-up and finally ravaged from within by a fire in 1959. Its bare interior preserves the scorch marks for posterity. Nearby, the nave of the now roofless Convento do Carmo was left unrestored after the 1755 disaster and looms over the city centre as a testament to that annus horribilis.

Lisbon's modern dereliction is hardly less striking. The Parque Mayer, hidden behind the Avenida da Liberdade, was opened in 1922 as a combination of amusement park and theatre district. Gradual decline resulted in its almost complete closure, although the art deco Teatro Capitólio was rebuilt and reopened last year. Further out is the glass-and-concrete Monsanto Panoramic Restaurant, a space-age rotunda that was designed in 1968 by Chaves da Costa. Derelict for more than a decade, its decaying murals and graffiti-covered walls still shelter some of the finest views over the city.

Museum piece
—
Paula Rego asked Eduardo Souto de Moura to design a "mischievous" building for her Casa das Histórias museum in Cascais. The rust-red concrete form with two pyramid-shaped towers appears as though made wholly from terracotta.
casadashistoriaspaularego.com

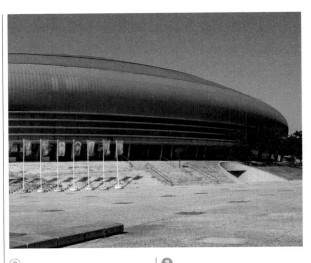

②
Meo Arena, Parque das Nações
Sing it

Portuguese architect Regino Cruz had the unenviable task of creating the country's largest indoor arena with minimal visual impact on the surrounding area. The result is this imposing structure, an immediate neighbourhood landmark, even though most think it more closely resembles a spacecraft than the intended upturned ship.

Lisboetas still generally refer to it as Pavilhão Atlântico; the current name reflects a sponsorship deal. It's the prime location for major concerts and international events such as conferences and summits.
Rossio dos Olivais, 1990-231
+ 351 21 891 8409
arena.meo.pt

Hold on, which city am I in?

③
Pavilhão do Conhecimento, Parque das Nações
In the know

In a prime location by the Rio Tejo, the Pavilion of Knowledge has been open to the public in its current state since 1999. Designed by Portuguese architect João Luís Carrilho da Graça, it features a suspended horizontal level, as well as an outdoor foyer leading to an entrance lined with grit sandstone.

Texture takes centre stage in this pavilion, with water features, smooth planes and lightly perforated walls allowing for controlled acoustics and lighting. Today it houses a science museum.
Largo José Mariano Gago, 1990-223
+ 351 21 891 7100
pavconhecimento.pt

Station master
—
The Gare do Oriente is now a destination in its own right

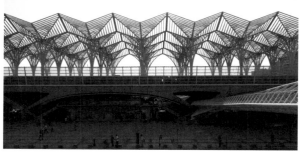

④
Gare do Oriente,
Parque das Nações
Airy structures

Completed for the 1998 World Expo, Santiago Calatrava's modernist masterpiece is a station like no other. Eight elevated train tracks and their corresponding platforms are covered by a massive metallic structure topped with an undulating steel-and-glass roof; for some observers it evokes a row of trees, for others the cloisters of an old gothic church.

Arriving into Portugal's biggest station – which caters for as many passengers as New York's Grand Central – makes for a stunning sight, both during the day and at night when the canopy is illuminated. By combining metro, train and bus routes, Gare do Oriente, which is opposite the Vasco da Gama shopping centre, has become a catalyst for urban renewal in the area.
Avenida Dom João II, 1990-233
carris.pt

Ponte 25 de Abril

If Lisbon's sunlight, steep inclines and recent positioning as a start-up capital don't conjure up images of an Iberian San Francisco, the Ponte 25 de Abril will. Connecting western Lisbon to the commuter town of Almada, it combines the vermillion hue of the Golden Gate with the form of San Francisco's other impressive span – the Bay Bridge – whose engineers were brought to Portugal to build it. Inaugurated in 1966 as the Ponte Salazar after the country's then dictator, the 2.3km-long crossing was renamed to commemorate the overthrow of his Estado Novo regime in 1974.

Lisbon has relatively few other bridges but the ones it does have are certainly spectacular. The Ponte Vasco da Gama, constructed for the 1998 World Expo, is the longest road bridge in Europe, spanning 12km across the wide Tejo estuary to the east of Lisbon. The Águas Livres Aqueduct, a triumph of 18th-century hydraulics that survived the 1755 earthquake, is even longer, measuring 14km. Designed to convey and control the city's capricious water sources, it was deactivated in the 1960s and now functions as a walkable monument.

Is it obvious that I can't see anything with these sunglasses on?

Modernism and postmodernism
Spaces of worship

Igreja de Nossa Senhora Auxiliadora, Prazeres
Divine inspiration

João Simões' 1964 Igreja de Nossa Senhora Auxiliadora is among the most attractive of the churches built under the deeply Catholic Estado Novo regime. Set in the Colégio dos Salesianos de Lisboa, its concrete-and-glass façade has a near baroque grandeur. The central concrete tower includes windows in the form of the cross, while curved sections behind boast an interlocking glass lattice. A pair of wing-like protrusions give the building an angelic appearance.

Inside, minimalism mingles with historical opulence: whitewashed walls, a soft, rounded ceiling and pinewood pews meet a fresco and plenty of stained glass.
34 Praça de São João Bosco, 1399-007
+351 21 090 0500
lisboa.salesianos.pt

②
Museu Calouste Gulbenkian,
Avenidas Novas
Comfort in concrete

Few concrete-and-glass structures
feel as welcoming as the original
Museu Calouste Gulbenkian,
home to the art collection of the
eponymous oil magnate (*see page
95*). Built in 1969 by competition-
winning architects Ruy Jervis
d'Athouguia, Pedro Cid and
Alberto Pessoa, its geometrically
simple T-shape belies the fluid
internal layout, decorated with
warm wooden furnishings.

Multiple terraces spill onto
one of Lisbon's finest landscaped
gardens, a place of undulating
topography, dense plantation and
wending waterways. The museum
and garden were designed in
dialogue: when the Gulbenkian
won the 1975 Valmor prize, the
architects were honoured alongside
landscape designers António Viana
Barreto and Gonçalo Ribeiro Telles.
*45A Avenida de Berna, 1067-001
+ 351 21 782 3461
gulbenkian.pt/museu*

119

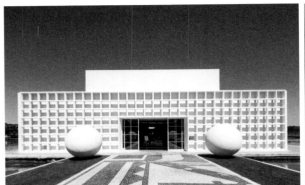

Palácio da Justiça, Avenidas Novas
Worth the wait

Back in 1962 the Portuguese government commissioned a pair of architects to build a new judicial headquarters. This plan fell through and Lisbon had to wait until 1970 for its Palácio da Justiça. Designed by Januário Godinho and João Andresen, the gargantuan brutalist structure hulks atop the Parque Eduardo VII. It would be interesting to know what the earlier architects would have made of it.

The bulk of the *palácio* consists of a colossal five-storey concrete block raised on a colonnaded ground floor, with sculptural square motifs under each window. Yet it's the northwestern end that's truly audacious, due to an elaborate pattern of recesses and a bulging appendage akin to a church transept; a monolithic service block sits at the northern tip. The overall construction forms a brutalist riot, a unique concatenation of unexpected parts.
Rua Marquês de Fronteira, 1098-001

③
Espaço Espelho d'Água, Belém
White noise

Approached across a moat, this is a rare remnant of the 1940 World Exhibition. It houses António Lino's dining pavilion, a whitewashed modernist quadrilateral with an otherwise simple structure that spotlights the drama of its recessed façade. It was marred by later ill-judged additions, until a 2014 restoration project by Duarte Caldas and Victor Vicente revived it as an art space and restaurant. Inside is a Sol LeWitt wall mural and a kitchen concealed by a vertical garden.
210 Avenida Brasília, 1400-038
+ 351 21 301 0510
espacoespelhodeagua.com

 ❹
Torres das Amoreiras, Campolide
Postmodern pioneer

Completed in 1985, this was Lisbon's first postmodern building complex and remains the most contentious. The work of architect Tomás Taveira, controversial for his salacious personal life and the alleged social problems in his housing projects, the three towers balance offices and apartments above a ground-level shopping mall. Taveira says that he designed them to evoke the helmets of medieval knights but their many elements (abstracted baroque cornices, Pombaline colonnades, Mies-like glass walls) congeal into a bewildering fusion of old and new.
32 Avenida Engenheiro Duarte Pacheco, 1070-103

Early 20th century
Headline acts

② **Antigo Hotel Vitória,**
Liberdade e Castilho
International style

Nestled among the functional
profiles of Avenida da Liberdade
is this masterpiece of art moderne.
Designed by architect Cassiano
Branco and erected in 1936,
Antigo Hotel Vitória has a façade
of curved balconies and minimal
blocks that bridges the luxury
of art deco and the rigour of the
International Style.

Conceived as an apartment
block but completed as a hotel,
during the Second World War it
became the haunt of German spies.
In recent times, its once-glamorous
suites have housed the offices of
the Portuguese Communist party.
170 Avenida da Liberdade, 1250-001

① **266 Avenida da Liberdade,**
Liberdade e Castilho
Stop the presses

Commonly called the Diário de
Noticias building, this landmark
was completed in 1940 by architect
Porfirio Pardal Monteiro. It was
the first structure specifically built
to house a newsroom in Portugal
and spans eight storeys, including
two underground floors for the
printing-press machines.

The newspaper's name perches
atop the façade in its traditional
gothic lettering; on the side, a
mosaic panel pays homage to the
world of print. After 76 years in
this location the newspaper found
a new home.
266 Avenida da Liberdade, 1250-096

*Well, how else am
I supposed to cope
with all these hills?*

Awe memorial
—
Based on a temporary
structure built for the 1940
World Exhibition, the huge
Padrão dos Descobrimentos
monument was unveiled
in 1960 to mark the 500th
anniversary of Henry the
Navigator's death.
padraodosdescobrimentos.pt

①

Casa dos Bicos, Alfama
Peculiar heritage

Constructed in the 16th century, this architectural curiosity gained its name, which roughly translates as "House of Spikes", from the 1,125 diamond-shaped stones that cover its façade. The building expertly combines this renaissance feature with a set of exuberant arched windows, typical of Portugal's Manueline style.

The Casa dos Bicos is one of the few structures that survived the devastating earthquake of 1755. When the city acquired the building in the 1960s and eventually began renovation works, remains from the Roman and Moorish periods were found. Today, after many years boarded up, the space is dedicated to the Nobel prize-winning Portuguese writer José Saramago and is once again open to the public – for a small admission fee.
10 Rua dos Bacalhoeiros, 1100-135
+351 21 880 2040
josesaramago.org

②

Elevador de Santa Justa, Baixa
Going up

This 1902 lift and beloved Lisbon landmark offers an alternative to the steep walk through Chiado, connecting downtown Baixa to the Largo do Carmo.

Its metallic neo-gothic style mirrors the work of Gustave Eiffel but in fact one of his students, the Portuguese engineer Raoul Mesnier du Ponsard, was responsible. Decorative openings in the cast-iron walls provide sweeping views on the ascent and, from the top floor, a spiral staircase leads to the even higher viewing platform, 32 metres above sea level.
Rua de Santa Justa, 1150-60
carris.pt

High marks
—
The Lisbon Valmor prize is one of Portugal's most renowned recognitions in the field of architecture. Since 1902 it's been attributed as a means to honour the best building or structure of each year. The lucky winner gets to add a plaque to its façade for posterity.

4

Fábrica de Cerâmica da Viúva
Lamego, Anjos
The extravaganza

The elaborate exterior of this
former tile-and-ceramics factory
turned shop is covered in intricate
tiles, all of which were handmade
when it was founded in 1849. The
front façade is clad in colourful
depictions of flowers and animals,
while other ornaments adorn door
and window frames. Above a small
art nouveau-style balcony a pair
of angels hold up the inscription
"Anno 1865": the year the shop
opened. A huge blue-and-white tile
panel covers the building's rear.
*25 Largo do Intendente Pina
Manique, 1100-285
viuvalamego.com*

③
Praça do Comércio, Baixa
Gateway to the city

Formerly the site of the Ribeira
Palace and still sometimes known
as the Terreiro do Paço, the Praça
do Comércio is the grand set piece
of the rebuilt downtown Baixa
area. Conceived by the Marquês de
Pombal, the square demonstrates
an austere yet elegant style in
contrast to the elaborate Manueline
façades of old Lisbon.

An equestrian statue of José I,
Pombal's patron, faces the river. In
1908 his descendant Carlos I was
assassinated while driving through
the square, an event that marked
the beginning of the end for the
Portuguese monarchy.
*1 Avenida Infante Dom Henrique,
1100-016*

Manueline style

Named after King Dom Manuel
I, the Manueline style combines
aspects of gothic architecture,
Spanish plateresque, Moorish
influence and a few Italian
touches. One of its main traits
is over-the-top ornamentation
that celebrates Portugal's
maritime heyday. Famed
examples still standing (many
Manueline structures were
wrecked in the 1775 quake)
include the stonework motifs
of the Torre de Belém and the
ornamentation adorning the
Mosteiro dos Jerónimos.

Sport and fitness
—— Onwards and upwards

It's almost impossible to come to Lisbon and not stretch your legs: wherever you are, you're going to have to wend your way up a crooked, cobbled hill – or seven.

Walking may be exercise enough for some but for those wanting to break a real sweat there are plenty of options. Though the bumpy terrain can make cycling and running tricky, in recent years the city has been linking its green spaces – the vast Parque Florestal de Monsanto in the western suburbs offers myriad cycling and running routes – and investing in a popular path along the waterfront. Plus, water is something the Portuguese capital has in abundance. Rent a boat and glide down the Rio Tejo or hop in a car and follow the river along the coast to the seaside village of Cascais, where you can surf the waves of the Atlantic Ocean.

We'll show you where to work out indoors and out. We'll also point you towards the top cutting-edge spas and old-school barbers when you want to kick back and relax.

Out and about
Breath of fresh air

①
The Four Seasons Hotel Ritz Spa, Avenidas Novas
On the run

The Four Seasons Hotel Ritz's rooftop fitness centre and basement spa can be accessed by non-guests between 06.30 and 22.30 for €150. The latter comprises a heated indoor pool, steam room and sauna. But the real treat is up top.

Perched on the roof is a glass-walled exercise room complete with treadmills, bikes and weights, as well as two studios (one for Pilates, the other for resistance training). The 400-metre U-shaped outdoor running track with views of the city is the jewel in the crown.
88 Rua Rodrigo da Fonseca, 1099-039
+ 351 21 381 1400
fourseasons.com/lisbon

BSpa by Karin Herzog, Belém
Treat yourself

Beneath the Altis Belém Hotel (*see page 19*) on the banks of the Rio Tejo, BSpa by Karin Herzog is a riverside retreat open to guests and non-guests from 09.00 to 21.00.

The tranquil Thermo Garden features a naturally lit indoor pool with waterfalls and a sundeck lined with chaises longues. There's also a marble-clad sauna, a Turkish bath and a nutritious menu by chef João Rodrigues. Treatments include the B Alive, a deep-tissue massage featuring bamboo sticks and rose oil, and both anti-ageing and deep-cleansing facials.
Doca do Bom Sucesso, 1400-038
+ 351 21 040 0220
altishotels.com

③
Sailing, Rio Tejo
Going with the flow

Traditional sailing boats were once a common sight on the Rio Tejo but today this blue expanse carries more huge cruise ships than *canoas* (canoes). It's still possible to get boating time in, however, thanks to several options, from kayaks to chartered yachts.

Seaventy runs short tours for small groups, with the option of an on-board lunch. If you're the skipper, RA Barcos rents out vessels at the Belém docks. The river gets choppy in the evening so set sail in the morning, taking in the city from the Torre de Belém to the Gare do Oriente (*see page 117*), passing under the Ponte 25 de Abril.
seaventy.pt; raboattours.com

Relax max
—
CitySpa in Restelo is an office-crowd favourite for the weekend unwind. Alongside exotic rituals and bamboo therapies, experts in shiatsu and reflexology are on-hand and Karin Herzog and Aromatherapy Associates products are stocked.
cityspa.pt

④
Surfing, region-wide
Catch a break

Lisbon has the best of both worlds: a vibrant metropolis and golden sandy beaches. Hop in a car and you'll soon be riding the Atlantic's breaks in a nearby coastal town.

A 20-minute drive west will take you to Estoril, where you'll find Carcavelos, São Pedro and Azarujinha beaches; all have reliable swells that are suitable for beginners. Guincho in the Parque Natural de Sintra-Cascais offers barrels for the more seasoned surfer. Beyond that is Ericeira, a fishing village and Europe's first World Surfing Reserve, with an array of great waves – beach breaks, point breaks and reef breaks – to suit all styles and abilities.

Football

Lisbon is home to two of the country's most famous football clubs: Benfica and Sporting Clube de Portugal (otherwise known as Sporting Lisbon). Their rivalry is fierce and well established: they first played each other in 1907 and between them have won 54 league titles, though Benfica have been in the ascendency in recent years.

While a class divide exists between the sides (Benfica's original stadium was built with fans' donations whereas la-di-da Sporting had royal backing), there's only about 3km between them geographically, so visiting both stadiums in an afternoon is very achievable. Both offer guided tours.

You could also watch a match, though the derby itself is nigh on impossible to get tickets for; the same goes for games against FC Porto, Portugal's other prominent team. Otherwise, either buy tickets online or at the ground – even on match day as neither team tends to sell out.
slbenfica.pt; sporting.pt

Grooming
Heads-up

①
Barbearia Campos, Chiado
Grooming

If it's time to get spruced up you'll have to take a seat, as was the case when Barbearia Campos first opened its doors in 1886. "It's not a long wait," says owner José Jorge Sá Chaves, whose ancestors founded this barbershop, Lisbon's oldest, right in the heart of Chiado.

The place feels as if it hasn't changed since then, with its horsehair brushes on the shelves and brown-leather chairs. There's an old ironing machine in the corner and newspaper clippings of famous customers hang on the wall. Its grooming services include moustache and beard trimming, as well as full close shaves.
4 Largo do Chiado, 1200-108
+351 21 342 8476

②
Barbearia Oliveira, Alfama
A cut above

Vintage-style barbershops are 10 a penny in Lisbon but Oliveira remains the prime salon for those craving a hot-towel shave while reclining in a Pessoa Lisboa antique chair. Brothers Bruno and Ângelo play up to the honky-tonk vibe, with tattooed forearms and the tools of their trade sported in pistol holsters. But the retro aesthetics don't detract from their handiwork.

Iconic products from Portugal – Antiga Barbearia de Bairro shaving cream, Semogue cherry-wood brushes and Musgo Real soap – complete the experience. A sister salon in Marvila services the art crowd.
27 Rua dos Remédios, 1100-441
+351 966 579 835

Three more esteemed barbers/hairdressers

01 Figaro's, Chiado
Figaro's is a traditional US-style barbershop with vintage barber chairs, old postcards on the walls and a beautiful tiled floor. It specialises in classic haircuts from the 1920s to the 1950s and barbers wearing bowler hats and braces perform hot-towel, straight-razor shaves.
figaroslisboa.com

02 Metrostudio, Baixa
Metrostudio individually tailors each grooming experience and offers personalised services such as cuts, colour and other hair treatments. Its stylists have experience in everything from TV work to international fashion weeks.
metrostudio.pt

03 Claus Porto, Chiado
Each Saturday, below luxury soap shop Claus Porto (*see page 48*), Salvador Rodrigues opens his small barbershop. Every aspect of his hot-towel shaves is designed to be relaxing, from the shop's marble-and-wood interior to the lavender-scented hot towels and the Musgo Real shaving products.
clausporto.com

Healthy change
—
Though offering all the standard spa therapies, Acqua Lisboa City Spa in Avenidas Novas is best known for its tailor-made body programmes that help with the long-term impacts of stress. The facial mesotherapy and acupuncture treatments are transformative.
acqualisboa.pt

Cycling route
Park and ride

Estrada do Outeiro

Rua Marquês
da Fronteira

Running route
Pound the city streets

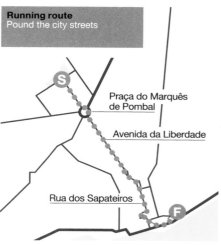

Praça do Marquês
de Pombal

Avenida da Liberdade

Rua dos Sapateiros

① Parque Florestal de Monsanto
Into the wild

Lisbon's largest green space is a peaceful and verdant expanse commanding beautiful views over the city.

STARTING POINT: Palácio da Justiça
DISTANCE: 15km

Start at the **①** *Palácio da Justiça* (*see page 120*), a brutalist structure from the 1960s, and follow red paved bike lanes to the outer reaches of the Parque Florestal de Monsanto. The area here is well-signposted and there are a number of bike trails to pick and choose from. For a simple route, head anticlockwise from the Parque do Calhau. There's a turning off to the 18th-century **②** *Águas Livres Aqueduct* but note that it leaves the park so turn back once you've taken in the vista.

Speaking of vistas, the Estrada da Bela Vista, west of the aqueduct, will take you uphill to the derelict Monsanto Panoramic Restaurant (*see page 116*), a spectacular 1960s artefact. Further south you can cross the motorway to visit the **③** *Pedreira dos Cactos* (Cactus Quarry) and the Montes Claros restaurant and gardens (a nice place for a break). There's also the Greek-style open-air **④** *Anfiteatro Keil do Amaral*, which has stunning views over the city.

Looping back to the north side of the motorway takes you to Estrada do Outeiro, which you can follow anticlockwise for about 5km back to the Parque do Calhau. From here on, it's red bike lanes back to the Palácio da Justiça.

① Park to river
Take in the sights

DISTANCE: 4.1km
GRADIENT: Downhill
DIFFICULTY: Easy
HIGHLIGHT: Many cultural and architectural landmarks
BEST TIME: Early morning, to avoid traffic and tourists
NEAREST METRO: Parque

Start at the Parque Eduardo VII viewpoint, next to the intriguing monument to the 25 April Revolution. Take the left-hand cobblestone path downhill. After some 600 metres you'll come to the *Praça do Marquês de Pombal*, where a monument honours the prime minister who rebuilt Lisbon following the 1755 quake.

Work around the roundabout until you reach the luxury shops of Avenida da Liberdade. Use one of the interior paths for about 1km down to the busy Praça dos Restauradores. Halfway through you'll have passed early 20th-century *Teatro Tivoli* on your left and modernist *Cinema São Jorge* (*see page 106*) to the right.

Pass Hotel Avenida Palace and turn left to *Teatro Nacional Dona Maria II* (*see page 104*). From the entrance, cross Praça do Rossio and take the tunnel under one of the 18th-century buildings. On the right you'll see Animatógrafo do Rossio, one of Lisbon's first cinemas, now showing X-rated films. At the end of the street, take a right to Rua Nova do Almada. Then turn left and immediately right to the *Museu do Dinheiro* (Money Museum). Next door is Praça do Município and city hall. Go around it to Rua do Arsenal.

Upon arrival at Praça do Comércio, the site of many ministry buildings, continue to the Arco da Rua Augusta. Take a right to *Cais das Colunas* (Columns Pier), Lisbon's historical gateway. Head left along the river for 300 metres. At Campo das Cebolas aim for Casa dos Bicos (*see page 122*), where the run ends.

Walks
— On the roads again

As you'll have gathered by now, Lisbon is a sprawling city built across a series of slopes – some gentle, others unforgiving. Still, what better way to explore than taking to the cobbled streets? From multicultural Mouraria and residential Campo de Ourique to artsy Marvila, architectural Parque das Nações and labyrinthine Alfama, each neighbourhood has a unique feel. Here are five routes to try – but don't be afraid to go off-piste.

NEIGHBOURHOOD 01

Mouraria
Multicultural past and present

This medieval quarter just north of downtown Baixa may not be as sophisticated as other central neighbourhoods but that's part of its charm. With a jumbled street layout and a long history as a multi-ethnic area, hilly Mouraria is brimming with hidden enclaves and, happily, has a slightly rundown feel.

Surrounding the west-facing walls of the Castelo de São Jorge, this is the area where the Moors were permitted to live after the Christian reconquest of the city in 1147 (before they and the Jews were expelled in 1497). It's also the spiritual home of the plaintive musical genre fado (*see page 103*): Portugal's most mythicised singer Maria Severa was born and raised here in the 1800s. From then on it was much neglected and gained a reputation for poverty and prostitution. However, since 2012 a series of urban-regeneration programmes have helped to create a cultural buzz, particularly in terms of nightlife and food. Despite the shiny new bars, the area has retained its bona fide ambience – although many residents are concerned by rising property prices.

More than 50 nationalities can be found living in this compact maze, making it a great place to grab a Bangladeshi snack, listen to some afro-house on a rooftop or simply soak up the street life where Portugal's most famous song was born.

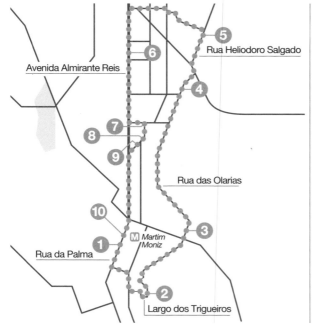

Avenida Almirante Reis

5 Rua Heliodoro Salgado

6

4

7

8

9

Rua das Olarias

10

M Martim Moniz

3

1

Rua da Palma

2

Largo dos Trigueiros

In at the steep end
Mouraria walk

This itinerary will take you from morning through to night, if you go about it at a leisurely pace, and encompasses all that Mouraria has to offer for those willing to put in the legwork. Start with a coffee on **1** *Praça Martim Moniz*, the home of Mercado de Fusão, which is a lively mixture of food stalls and cultural events at weekends. Residents from all walks of life come to hang out next to the

Address book

01 Praça Martim Moniz
1100-341
02 Camilla Watson Studio
16A Largo dos Trigueiros,
1100-246
+351 21 131 2488
camillawatsonphotography.
net
03 Mariza's house
Travessa dos Lagares,
1100-300
04 Mercado do Forno
do Tijolo
5 Rua Maria da Fonte,
1170-220
05 Miradouro do Monte
Agudo
Rua Heliodoro Salgado,
1170-170
06 Paróquia de Nossa
Senhora dos Anjos
Avenida Almirante Reis,
1170-286
07 Largo Café Estúdio
19 Largo do Intendente,
1100-285
+351 21 888 5420
08 Casa Independente
45 Largo do Intendente,
1100-285
+351 21 887 2842
casaindependente.com
09 Infame
4 Largo do Intendente,
1100-285
+351 21 880 4008
infame.pt
10 Topo
Commercial Center Martim
Moniz, Praça Martim
Moniz, 1100-341
+351 21 588 1322

slightly surreal modern fountains, the main one referencing the ancient wall that ran from this part of town up to the castle.

Walk towards downtown and take a left up the steep stone steps to Largo dos Trigueiros, a charming square where you'll find ② *Camilla Watson Studio*. Based here since 2007, the UK-born artist's photography celebrates the elderly residents of Mouraria and can be found adorning the streets in a kind of open-air gallery. Keep an eye out for her black-and-white images as you head north, climbing more winding steps, and follow Rua do Marquês de Ponte de Lima until you hit Travessa dos Lagares. Fans of fado today should look out for the pink façade of ③ *Mariza's house*. This is where contemporary fado singer Mariza was born and is a reminder of how significant this neighbourhood is to the genre.

Turn left at the end of the street and continue through a quiet, residential thoroughfare until you reach ④ *Mercado do Forno do Tijolo*, a modernist project created by architect Eduardo dos Reis and

built in 1956. It's still used as a food market, as well as a cultural-design hub thanks to the presence of digital-manufacturing laboratory FabLab Lisboa. After exploring, continue along the same road, bearing left when you hit Rua do Forno do Tijolo and then taking the first right. Continue until you reach ⑤ *Miradouro do Monte Agudo*, one of Lisbon's calmer *esplanadas* (terraces), where you can reward yourself with a drink and impressive views.

Exit down some steps then follow Rua de Cabo Verde to the left, taking a right and heading down Rua de Angola through the Bairro das Colónias. When you hit the metro stop Anjos turn left onto the neighbourhood's main street, Avenida Almirante Reis. You'll soon come to ⑥ *Paróquia de Nossa Senhora dos Anjos*, a church with a rebuilt neoclassical façade whose interiors, including the gilded woodwork, hark back to the 1600s – with paintings from a century earlier.

Continue along the main street then take a left into Largo do Intendente, a historical square. Grab a souvenir at A Vida Portuguesa (*see page 49*) then choose between the following: ⑦ *Largo Café Estúdio*, which serves simple lunches on its terrace; ⑧ *Casa Independente*, a creatively minded and rambling space that's perfect for a pre-dinner drink (or a late dance); and ⑨ *Infame*, which serves global cuisine in an art nouveau hotel.

If, after all of the above, you still have the energy, continue south to Praça Martim Moniz and grab a drink at ⑩ *Topo*, a rooftop bar housed above a shopping mall.

Getting there

Mouraria is well served by the *verde* (green) metro line, with Martim Moniz station located under the main square. The famous Tram 28 also starts and ends here but is way too crowded unless it's very early in the morning. If you're staying in the centre, walking here is best.

NEIGHBOURHOOD 02

Campo de Ourique
Picturesque splendour

This walk, which takes in two cemeteries, the Portuguese parliament, a church rooftop, parks and plenty of coffee shops along the way, covers one of Lisbon's leafiest and most bourgeois historic suburbs.

Back when the likes of Alfama and Mouraria were poor fishing and immigrant *bairros*, Campo de Ourique and neighbouring Príncipe Real housed merchants and princes. The area survived the earthquake of 1755 and Campo de Ourique entered the history books when it became the centre of the revolutionary movement that overthrew the monarchy and led to the formation of the Portuguese Republic. A plaque on a building in the area (a short detour from this walk at 93 Rua Campo de Ourique) commemorates the morning of 4 October 1910, when the group of "civil revolutionaries" left the house to oversee the coup d'état that led to the establishment of the republic the following day.

Today there is no hint of revolutionary agitation in this pretty, bustling neighbourhood. Campo de Ourique remains quietly wealthy and has managed to avoid becoming too touristy. Of course, there's a growing influx of foreign residents, particularly French, drawn by its shops and markets, which continue to trade on charming streets.

Get down to it
Campo de Ourique walk

Take Tram 28 to the end of the line and start at ❶ *Cemitério dos Prazeres*, the largest cemetery in Lisbon and the final resting place of many stately Portuguese families, artists and writers. It's open to visitors and its tree-lined lanes of tombs and mausoleums – some the size of small chapels – are worth a short wander.

Leaving the cemetery, turn left and then right onto Rua Padre Francisco, where you'll find ❷ *Mercado de Campo de Ourique*. This former neighbourhood market is now brimming with food stalls so there are plenty of options for a snack or meal. If you're in the mood for something sweet, just outside on Rua Tenente Ferreira Durão is ❸ *O Melhor Bolo de Chocolate do Mundo* (The Best Chocolate Cake in the World).

Exit the market on the opposite side from which you entered, onto Rua Coelho da Rocha. Here you'll find ❹ *Casa Fernando Pessoa*, the house where Portuguese poet

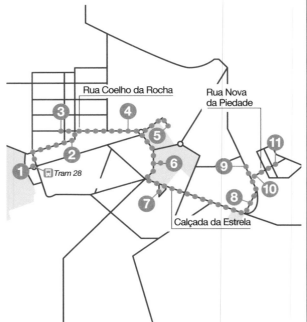

Rua Coelho da Rocha

Rua Nova da Piedade

❸

❹

❺

❶ ▣ *Tram 28*

❷

❻

⑪

❾

❿

❼

❽

Calçada da Estrela

Fernando Pessoa lived for the last 15 years of his life. Today it's a museum, inviting visitors to observe the poet's bedroom and workspace from Monday to Saturday.

On leaving the museum, turn left and then right onto Rua Silva Carvalho and walk down to the large roundabout. The next three stops are all visible from here: ⑤ *Cemitério dos Ingleses* on the left, ⑥ *Jardim da Estrela* in front and ⑦ *Basílica da Estrela* to the right.

The Cemitério dos Ingleses, open mornings from Monday

to Friday, dates back to the 18th century. It was the place of burial for those British residents of the city who were Anglicans, and as such not buried in the same cemeteries as Catholics. It has lush gardens and one famous resident: novelist Henry Fielding, author of *Tom Jones*, died in Lisbon in 1754.

Jardim da Estrela is one of Lisbon's most beautiful parks, with a small pond, an outdoor café, a bandstand and, intriguingly, a tiny kiosk-library. Open from 13.00 to 17.00, the latter

dispenses newspapers, books and periodicals.

Across the street, Basílica da Estrela, constructed in 1790, is a city landmark. Climb a set of steep stairs to its roof for great views of the city, the castle, the river and Ponte 25 de Abril (*see page 118*). There's also a vertigo-inducing balcony that offers views into the church below. Almost always empty, it's one of the most peaceful viewpoints in Lisbon.

It's a steep walk down Calçada da Estrela, past the prime minister's residence on the right, to ⑧ *Assembleia da República*. Built in 1615 as a monastery, it was damaged by the 1755 earthquake and, following the Liberal Revolution of 1820 and the dissolution of the religious orders in 1834, taken over as the parliament building.

Walk across the plaza, head down the steps at the far end and cross Rua de São Bento. Here you'll find a row of unassuming shops. Take a peek inside ⑨ *Depósito da Marinha Grande*, the outlet for glass company Marinha Grande, which has been producing distinctive hand-blown glass since 1769.

Turn right onto Rua Nova da Piedade and reward yourself with a gelato at ⑩ *Gelataria Nannarella*. There's usually a queue (worth joining) for the daily and weekly specials. If ice cream isn't your thing, a short walk on the same side of the road brings you to ⑪ *Copenhagen Coffee Lab* (*see page 42*), a sleek café with great coffee and fresh cinnamon buns. End the walk at Praça das Flores, a small square with a pretty fountain.

Address book

01 Cemitério dos Prazeres
Praça São João Bosco,
1350-297
+351 21 396 1511

02 Mercado de Campo de Ourique
104 Rua Coelho da Rocha,
1350-075
+351 21 132 3701

03 O Melhor Bolo de Chocolate do Mundo
62A Rua Tenente Ferreira Durão, 1350-008
+351 21 396 5372
omelhorbolodechocolate
domundobycbl.com

04 Casa Fernando Pessoa
16 Rua Coelho da Rocha,
1250-088
+351 21 391 3270
casafernandopessoa.cm-
lisboa.pt

05 Cemitério dos Ingleses
Avenida Álvares Cabral,
1250-235
lisbonanglicans.org

06 Jardim da Estrela
Praça da Estrela, 1200-667
+351 21 397 4818

07 Basílica da Estrela
Praça da Estrela, 1200-667
+351 21 396 0915

08 Assembleia da República
Rua de São Bento,
1249-068
+351 21 391 9000

09 Depósito da Marinha Grande
234 Rua São Bento,
1200-821
+351 21 396 3234
dmg.com.pt

10 Gelataria Nannarella
64 Rua Nova da Piedade,
1200-263
+351 926 878 553
nannarella.pt

11 Copenhagen Coffee Lab
10 Rua Nova da Piedade,
1200-298
+351 916 604 054
cphcoffeelab.pt

NEIGHBOURHOOD 03

Marvila

Watch this space

With its vast warehouses, industrial architecture and river views, it's no wonder that Lisbon's eastern neighbourhood of Marvila is undergoing a cultural regeneration. But it's only recently that the potential of the old dockside spaces has been recognised. This area, between the historic city centre and sleek Parque das Nações, has long laid unnoticed so is still (fairly) free of tourists.

The port zone started out as an agricultural area in the 16th century – with working farms, wineries and convents – and went on to become the manufacturing heart of the city in the mid-19th century. After a period of decline the factories were forgotten and the wine and weapon warehouses became disused. The turnaround began in 2007 when lecturer Nuno Nabais transformed the former arms factory Fábrica Braço de Prata into a cultural centre supporting Portuguese artists, musicians and writers. In 2009 gallerist Andréa Baginski Champalimaud followed suit and today there's a handful of cutting-edge contemporary-art galleries between the derelict buildings.

This walk is best undertaken in the afternoon – most galleries are open from 14.00 but check before you set off – and will take you to vast white-walled spaces, quirky cultural centres, bustling craft breweries and late-night bars. Escape the crowds and soak up the city's creative buzz.

Culture, cocktails and craft beer
Marvila walk

Your walk begins with a journey through the history of Portuguese tiles at the **1** *Museu Nacional do Azulejo* (*see page 93*) in the former convent of Madre de Deus. Once you've had your fill, exit left onto Rua de Xabregas, continuing straight over the junction before crossing to the right-hand side of the road. Opposite the Teatro Ibérico take the right fork onto Rua da Manutenção,

admiring Lithuanian artist Ernest Zacharevic's quadriptych of a girl in a blue dress on your left. Ahead is **2** *Restaurante Marítima de Xabregas*, just in time for a late lunch; we recommend the *filetes de peixe-galo* (dory fish fillets).

Appetite sated, exit right, then bear left and continue along Rua da Manutenção to **3** *Galeria Filomena Soares*. Behind the pink façade are two vast spaces that host exhibitions and events. Cross the street and head down the road to the left, which leads back to Rua de Xabregas. Turn right and continue, passing a handful of convenience stores and a painted wall of hand-holding children. Soon you'll see (and perhaps hear, depending on the time of day) the baroque Convento do Grilo on your left.

Cross the road but continue straight on what has become Rua do Grilo, passing a military zone (we told you this neighbourhood was different) and a couple of restaurants. Soon you'll reach a pretty square surrounded by colourful houses. Walk around it, taking in the tiled buildings to your

left, then head along Rua do Grilo, which becomes Rua do Beato.

Just before you reach the end of the car park, turn left down Rua José Domingos Barreiros, then turn right onto Rua Capitão Leitão. Pull up a pew at Lisbon's first craft brewery, ❹ *Dois Corvos Cervejeira*, then continue along Rua Capitão Leitão, crossing the street to ❺ *Galeria Baginski*. Opened in 2009 by Andréa Baginski Champalimaud, this was one of the first galleries to move to the area. Since then others have followed, including ❻ *Galeria Francisco Fino* (*see page 99*), which opened across the street in 2017.

Continue to the end, turn right and ahead you'll see ❼ *Bar Capitão Leitão*, a cocktail bar complete with a mini record shop. Be sure to visit the Mexican-themed bathroom then exit right and continue to the end, back onto Rua do Açúcar. Opposite is another craft brewery, ❽ *Cerveja Musa*, housed in a century-old red-brick warehouse that was once used for drying chestnuts. Here you can either taste or take home fresh brews.

Getting there
___
Buses 210, 718, 742, 794 and 759 (the latter only at night) stop outside the Museu Nacional do Azulejo, while 728 and 759 stop on nearby Avenida Infante Dom Henrique. Santa Apolónia station is a 20-minute walk away; there's also a car park in front of the museum.

Continue along Rua do Açúcar until you reach interior designer Rita Estanislau's ❾ *Café com Calma* (*see page 42*). You may not need refuelling again but this eclectic establishment serves everything from salads to cake and makes a mean lemonade. Exit left, continuing into another tree-lined square, then cross to the right and follow the right fork past El Bulo Social Club and Lisbon WorkHub. After a few minutes cross the street, glancing right at the river, onto Rua Fernando Palha.

Head past the black-and-white sign to Fábrica Braço de Prata and cross a fairly busy road, continuing to ❿ *Underdogs Gallery* (*see page 101*), an exhibition space dedicated to urban-inspired contemporary artists. Finally, head back the way you came, taking a left onto Rua da Fábrica de Material de Guerra to the aforementioned ⓫ *Fábrica Braço de Prata* (*see page 102*), an arts and culture centre with a bar that's open until late. Leaf through the books in the library and take in the artwork on show before settling down with a drink.

Address book

01 Museu Nacional do Azulejo
4 Rua Madre de Deus, 1900-312
+351 21 810 0340
museudoazulejo.gov.pt

02 Restaurante Marítima de Xabregas
40 Rua da Manutenção, 1900-320
+351 21 868 2235
restaurantemaritimade xabregas.com.pt

03 Galeria Filomena Soares
80 Rua da Manutenção, 1900-321
+351 21 862 4122
gfilomenasoares.com

04 Dois Corvos Cervejeira
94 Rua Capitão Leitão, 1950-052
+351 914 440 326
doiscorvos.pt

05 Galeria Baginski
51-53 Rua Capitão Leitão, 1950-050
+351 21 397 0719
baginski.com.pt

06 Galeria Francisco Fino
76 Rua Capitão Leitão, 1950-052
+351 925 623 717
franciscofino.com

07 Bar Capitão Leitão
5B Rua Capitão Leitão, 1950-013
+351 21 580 9594

08 Cerveja Musa
83 Rua do Açúcar, 1950-006
+351 21 387 7777
cervejamusa.com

09 Café com Calma
10 Rua do Açúcar, 1950-242
+351 21 868 0398

10 Underdogs Gallery
56 Rua Fernando Palha, 1950-132
+351 21 868 0462
under-dogs.net

11 Fábrica Braço de Prata
1 Rua da Fábrica de Material de Guerra, 1950-128
+351 965 518 068
bracodeprata.com

NEIGHBOURHOOD 04

Parque das Nações
Banish boredom

Parque das Nações (or Expo, as Lisboetas call it) is Lisbon's most northeastern neighbourhood and a relatively young part of the city: it was created in 1998 by combining parts of three different parishes for the grounds of that year's World Fair. After the fair left town the park underwent a transformation, making use of the myriad structures that were left behind (*see page 115*). Its architecture stands in contrast to that of Lisbon's city centre, with modernist works by architects such as Portugal's Álvaro Siza Vieira and Spain's Santiago Calatrava, and water features along the riverfront nod to the fair's oceanic theme.

Today this new urban district is one of the most sought-after postcodes in the city, with a plethora of green spaces and an off-the-beaten-track entertainment hub. From a modern casino to a state-of-the-art oceanarium and Lisbon's main live-music venue, the Meo Arena, you'll never be bored. Plus, countless bars and restaurants provide privileged views across the Rio Tejo and towards the stunning Ponte Vasco da Gama, one of Europe's longest bridges at 17km.

Perfect for a morning jog, lounging in one of the sun-drenched gardens or a Sunday-afternoon stroll, Parque das Nações shows how a World Fair can be done right – revitalising an entire wedge of a city in the process.

Architecture and riverside views
Parque das Nações

The starting point for this walk is easy to find: 145 metres above the ground stands the **1** *Torre Vasco da Gama*, one of the tallest structures in Lisbon. Built in 1998 for the World Fair and named after the renowned Portuguese explorer, its steel shape resembles the sail of a caravel (a small and speedy Portuguese sailing ship from the 15th to 17th centuries) in a nod to the country's Age of Discovery.

If you want to soak up the stunning riverside views and take the weight off your feet, this is also where you'll find the entrance to **2** *Telecabine Lisboa*, an urban cable car that runs along the entire length of the park (and most of this walk) during an eight-minute ride. It's fairly low-profile – and low to the ground – so keep your eyes peeled.

Now back to the point of this chapter: walking. Head towards the green **3** *Jardim Garcia de Orta*, which is home to five unique gardens. Stroll down Passeio das Tágides, enjoying the different ecosystems. You'll find plants and flowers from the former colonies of São Tomé and Príncipe, Goa, Macau and Cape Verde, as well as from the Portuguese archipelagos of the Azores and Madeira. Take a break midway at restaurant **4** *BoaLisboa* for a relaxed lunch of hearty traditional Portuguese food plated by Michelin-starred chef Maria Gomes.

After lunch continue through the gardens until you reach the **5** *Lago das Tágides*. It's a series of sculptures by Portuguese artist

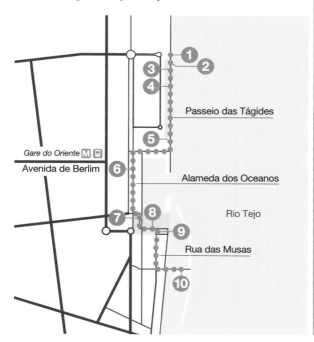

Passeio das Tágides

Gare do Oriente M 🚌
Avenida de Berlim

Alameda dos Oceanos

Rio Tejo

Rua das Musas

João Cutileiro that appear to float on the water; they illustrate the nymphs of the Tejo as imagined by poet Luís de Camões.

Continue along the riverfront and take a right turn at Rossio dos Olivais, where the flags of all attending countries of the 1998 World Fair are still proudly on display. Remember to look down as well as up: this avenue features the Mar Largo (Wide Ocean) pavement style, one of the most popular cobblestone designs shaped with intersecting waves.

Before turning left onto Alameda dos Oceanos take a moment to appreciate "Homem Sol" (Sun Man), a steel sculpture by Portuguese artist Jorge Vieira that is one of the greatest pieces of public art on display in the city.

Continue and on your left you'll find the **6** *Pavilhão de Portugal* (*see page 115*), designed by Pritzker prize-winning architect Álvaro Siza Vieira. Based on a sheet of paper balancing on two bricks, it features an impressive gravity-defying sagging roof. From the pavilion,

carry on towards the **7** *Pavilhão do Conhecimento* (*see page 116*), a science-and-technology museum housed in a Valmor prize-winning building. This place is perfect for children because most of its exhibitions are interactive.

Exit towards the **8** *Jardins da Água* and explore this water-themed green space, an ideal spot in which to cool off in summer. Make your way to the riverfront and on your right you'll spot the **9** *Teatro Camões*. One of the most prestigious cultural institutions in the city, this is the headquarters of the National Ballet Company and a venue where some of the best performances in the country take place.

Feeling thirsty? After a show head to Rua das Musas and then turn left on Passeio do Adamastor towards **10** *Lisboa Marina*. Make a beeline for the restaurant's roof terrace and sip a glass of chilled white port before dinner. Sit back and relax: you should have arrived just in time for sunset.

Getting there

Hop on the *vermelha* (red) metro line to Santiago Calatrava's Gare do Oriente (pausing to admire its open-air platforms and striking modern design). Alternatively, hitch a ride on the 705, 708, 725 or 744 buses.

Address book

01 Torre Vasco da Gama
Cais das Naus, 1990-173
+351 21 891 8409
portaldasnacoes.pt

02 Telecabine Lisboa
Passeio das Tágides, 1990-280
+351 21 895 6143
telecabinelisboa.pt

03 Jardim Garcia de Orta
Rua da Pimenta, 1990-096
+351 21 891 8409
portaldasnacoes.pt

04 BoaLisboa
75 Rua da Pimenta, 1990-254
+351 937 758 003
boalisboa.pt

05 Lago das Tágides
Passeio das Tágides, 1990-221
+351 21 891 8409
portaldasnacoes.pt

06 Pavilhão de Portugal
Alameda dos Oceanos, 1990-221
+351 21 891 8409
portaldasnacoes.pt

07 Pavilhão do Conhecimento
Largo José Mariano Gago, 1990-223
+351 21 891 7100
pavconhecimento.pt

08 Jardins da Água
Passeio de Ulisses, 1990-005
+351 21 891 8409
portaldasnacoes.pt

09 Teatro Camões
Passeio do Neptuno, 1990-193
+351 21 892 3470
cnb.pt

10 Lisboa Marina
2F, Edifício Nau, Passeio do Adamastor, 1990-007
+351 914 037 068
lisboamarina.pt

NEIGHBOURHOOD 05

Alfama
Go off-guide

Scrambling down a vertiginous hillside from the toothy Castelo de São Jorge to the glittering Rio Tejo, Alfama is a far cry from the orderly grid of Baixa below. Here you'll find a tangled knot of streets, poky pastel-coloured squares and charming *miradouros* (lookout points) that echo with the sound of fado and caged songbirds.

Originally settled in the Iron Age and later occupied by the Romans, Visigoths and Moors, this is the oldest area in the city. Due to its dense bedrock foundations, much of it survived the disastrous 1755 earthquake relatively unscathed and it's here that you'll find the only known Roman amphitheatre in Portugal. Drowsy cats laze in doorways, implausibly attractive laundry flutters from balconies and Tram 28 clatters up and down the cobbles through the neighbourhood's heart, carrying its ceaseless consignment of camera-wielding sightseers.

This walk winds its way from the city's 12th-century cathedral to one of our favourite vantage points (via a watering hole or two) but we suggest that you use our itinerary merely as a guide: Alfama's charms arguably lie in chance discoveries. So stick this book in your backpack and allow yourself to get a little lost – we won't be offended.

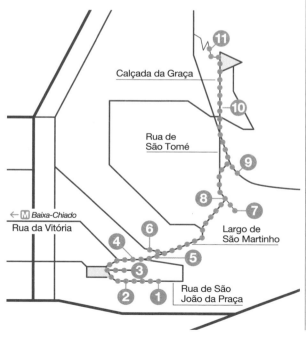

Historic highlights
Alfama walk

Start your walk with a caffeine hit under the arches of ❶ *Pois Café* (you're going to need it). The sofas might be inviting and the atmosphere relaxed but don't get too comfortable: those cobbles aren't going to conquer themselves. If you find yourself in need of additional fuel, turn left out of the café, past the orange trees that hug the base of the towering cathedral walls along Cruzes da Sé, and

stop at ❷ *Ao Pé da Sé*. Grab a seat outside and order a fresh salad.

After lunch follow the road round to the right past the chunky towers of the ❸ *Sé de Lisboa*. Construction of Lisbon's cathedral began after the reconquest in 1147 on the site of the city's main mosque and the robust structure has survived numerous earthquakes. Peek inside before taking a right and heading up Rua Augusto Rosa past the ❹ *Museu do Aljube*. This museum documenting Portugal's recent political history and the Salazar regime (one of the longest dictatorships in European history) is housed in what was once Salazar's secret police prison.

Carry on up the street, perhaps ducking into ❺ *ChiCoração* to admire its Portuguese woollen clothes and blankets. Then take the first left, Rua da Saudade, to peer over the railings at what remains of the ❻ *Teatro Romano*, which once seated 4,000 people. The site was discovered in 1798 during the reconstruction of the city after the earthquake of 1755. To find out more about the history of Olisipo,

as the outpost city was known in Emperor Augustus's day, pop into the museum opposite.

Retrace your steps to Rua Augusto Rosa, a street that changes name so frequently along its winding incline that locals often refer to it simply as Rua do Eléctrico da Sé, after the famous tram that rattles up and down it. Continue up the hill past a colossal thick-trunked *phytolacca dioica* (ombú) tree.

Dip your toes in the wading pool by the trellises of the Miradouro de Santa Luzia on the right but before you get too enthusiastic about the view, continue round the corner to ⑦ *Miradouro das Portas do Sol*. You won't have it to yourself but in a city packed with superlative vistas this is arguably the most arresting. Behind you, on the edge of the square, is the ⑧ *Fundação Ricardo do Espírito Santo Silva*. Also known as the Museu-Escola de Artes Decorativas, this 17th-century palace houses a collection of 16th to 19th-century Portuguese, French and English furniture, tapestries, silverware and antiques.

Getting there
—
Tram 28 frequently bustles past the steps of the Sé in both directions but you'll have to battle for a spot. The nearest metro stop to Pois Café is Baixa-Chiado, which is roughly 10 minutes away by foot – the perfect warm up.

If you're still with us, carry on along the street (which, after a few more name changes, has become Rua de São Tomé), following it round to the right (downhill, briefly) until it morphs into Escolas Gerais. On the left you'll find ⑨ *Os Gazeteiros*, a restaurant run by French chef David Eyguesier, who cut his teeth at Pois Café (he never went to culinary school; the restaurant's name loosely translates as "the truants"). Eyguesier's organic dishes change daily.

After dinner turn right out of the restaurant and on the corner take Rua do Salvador. Continue up the street until it forks and turn right onto Calçada da Graça. Here you'll find ⑩ *Graça do Vinho*, a wine bar in a former pharmacy serving Portuguese plonk by the glass or bottle.

If you've got the energy after your nightcap, turn right out of the bar and drag yourself up to the ⑪ *Miradouro Sophia de Mello Breyner Andresen* (named after a Portuguese poet) to watch the lights flickering over the city all the way to the Ponte 25 de Abril.

Address book

01 Pois Café
93-95 Rua São João da Praça, 1100-521
+351 21 886 2497
poiscafe.com

02 Ao Pé da Sé
31 Rua Cruzes da Sé, 1100-585
+351 21 886 0655

03 Sé de Lisboa
Largo da Sé, 1100-585
+351 21 886 6752
patriarcado-lisboa.pt

04 Museu do Aljube
42 Rua Augusto Rosa, 1100-091
+351 21 817 2400
museudoaljube.pt

05 ChiCoração
22 Rua Augusto Rosa, 1100-059
+351 969 307 096
chicoracao.pt

06 Teatro Romano
6 Rua de São Mamede, 1100-059
+351 21 581 8530
museudelisboa.pt

07 Miradouro das Portas do Sol
Largo das Portas do Sol, 1100-411

08 Fundação Ricardo do Espírito Santo Silva
2 Largo das Portas do Sol, 1100-411
+351 21 881 4600
fress.pt

09 Os Gazeteiros
114-116 Rua das Escolas Gerais, 1100-220
+351 21 886 0399
osgazeteiros.pt

10 Graça do Vinho
10A Calçada da Graça, 1100-266
+351 21 011 8041

11 Miradouro Sophia de Mello Breyner Andresen
Calçada da Graça, 1100-265

Resources
— Inside knowledge

We've shown you where to pick up the tastiest *pastéis de nata*, been particular about funiculars and brought you all the history we can find. We've wended our way along the city's cobbled streets and highlighted our favourite museums, restaurants and shops – as well as the best bars for a pre- or post-dinner shot of *ginjinha*.

Now all you need to know is how to navigate the city. Whether that's via train, tram, taxi or on foot, remember to bring your walking shoes. We also have suggestions for outdoor and indoor activities (not that you should expect much rain in one of Europe's sunniest capitals), a list of our favourite events taking place in Lisbon and a selection of tunes to provide an authentic soundtrack to your trip.

Transport
Get around town

01 Flights: Lisbon's airport is a mere 15-minute drive from the city centre. The metro red line takes you to Alameda in 20 minutes (change to the green line here and you'll be in the centre in no time). There's also an express airport bus from central stops and a taxi costs about €15.

02 Metro and trains: The metro runs between 06.30 and 01.00 but it isn't extensive and, particularly on the green line, is often crowded. Singles cost €1.45, while dailies are €6.15. Overground trains are the quickest and easiest way to reach Cascais (depart from Cais do Sodré) and Sintra (depart from Rossio); singles cost €2.15. *metrolisboa.pt; cp.pt*

03 Trams: Lisbon's trams are an integral part of the cityscape. Tourists love the 28, which heads through the historic heart of the city, but be aware that it's not a Disney ride: residents on a daily commute can get understandably frustrated when being jostled by visitors trying to take photographs.

04 On foot: Lisbon is a small city and exploring on foot is the best way to discover the quiet back lanes and pretty squares that lend it its charm. All you need are sensible shoes and a decent level of fitness to master the hills.

05 Bikes: The city isn't bicycle friendly, either in terrain (steep cobbled streets) or culture (drivers aren't used to cyclists). Unless you're on the riverside cycle path or in the university district, it's best to give bikes a miss.

06 Taxis: Taxis are affordable. Rides start at €3.42, with a kilometre rate of 47 cents, and you're unlikely to spend more than €10 on a city-centre journey. For a private vehicle book with Blacklane. *blacklane.com*

Vocabulary
Local lingo

This list of terms will help you navigate the linguistic landscape.

01 Obrigado: Thank you (women say *obrigada*)
02 Bom dia: Good morning
03 Boa tarde/boa noite: Good afternoon/good night
04 Bica: Espresso
05 Imperial: Small draft beer
06 Tudo bem? Literally, "Everything well?" Asked whenever you meet someone
07 A conta: The bill
08 Pois: A word of agreement, pronounced "poish", used regularly to encourage the conversation
09 Lanche: Not lunch, not dinner but that vital late-afternoon snack
10 Vinho verde: Literally "green wine" but better translated as "young wine". It's usually white with a slight spritz

Soundtrack to the city
Top tunes

01 Carlos do Carmo, 'Lisboa Menina e Moça': Portugal's most famous living fado singer's ode to Lisbon.
02 Madredeus, 'Alfama': A tune by perhaps the best-known modern Portuguese band. It features in Wim Wenders' *Lisbon Story*.
03 Dead Combo, 'Lisboa Mulata': Guitar duo with a contemporary-pop edge.
04 Mariza, 'Fado em Mim': Credited with revitalising fado for a new generation, this Mozambique-born singer has sold more than one million records.
05 Buraka Som Sistema, 'Black Diamond': This group reflects the new sounds emerging from Lisbon's poorer *bairros*, fusing African zouk and kuduro with techno and highlighting the city's multicultural heart.

Sunny days
The great outdoors

Sunny days abound in Lisbon but, thanks to the river and sea breezes, it's rarely unbearably hot. Wandering along the back lanes of Alfama and Príncipe Real, taking your time to sit in the shade and drink a cold beer or two, is pretty much the perfect way to enjoy summer in the city.

01 Ferry ride: Head to Cais do Sodré ferry port and catch one of the commuter ferries to Cacilhas on the other side of the river, where you'll find a wide selection of seafood restaurants that also serve Portuguese sparkling wine. Take a walk along the waterfront up the lift that carries you to Almada and offers great views of Lisbon. You can also hop on a bus in Cacilhas and visit the iconic "Cristo Rei" statue.

02 Cascais and Estoril: About 30 minutes by train from Cais do Sodré are the coastal villages of Cascais and Estoril. The beaches can be crowded on weekends but during the week they're a great place to escape for some sun and a swim. Cascais is a pretty village with plenty of lunch spots and is also home to Santini ice-cream parlour. For those with more upmarket tastes, Estoril has a casino and a regal reputation.

03 'Miradouro' and kiosk tour: Lisbon has a plethora of squares and parks, many of which have beautiful views and almost all of which have a bustling kiosk or café. On a hot day they're the perfect refreshment stops. Our favourites include Jardim do Príncipe Real, which is shady and ideal for a post-shopping revival; Miradouro da Graça on the Tram 28 line, with its sweeping views over the city; and Adamastor, in Bica, where the hippy kids hang out.

Rainy days
Weather-proof activities

Lisbon is one of Europe's sunniest capitals, with more than 250 rain-free days a year. January to April are the wettest months but even then it very rarely rains all day. Plan one of the activities below and by the time you emerge there's every chance the sun will be out.

01 Museu Calouste Gulbenkian: This museum (see pages 95 and 119) houses an eclectic collection of Egyptian, Greek, Roman, Islamic, Asian and European art amassed over 40 years by oil magnate Calouste Gulbenkian. There's also a gallery dedicated to modern Portuguese art. The building, designed by Ruy Jervis d'Athouguia, Pedro Cid and Alberto Pessoa, is one of Lisbon's modern gems. There are also picturesque gardens if the sun decides to reappear.
gulbenkian.pt

02 Oceanarium: Housed in Lisbon's Expo zone, Parque das Nações (see page 134), this is especially good if you're travelling with kids. But, with more than 450 species of marine life, there's plenty to entertain adults too. Nearby are some fine examples of contemporary architecture, including Santiago Calatrava's Gare do Oriente (see page 117).
oceanario.pt

03 Belém: Packed with museums and galleries, Belém is the perfect rainy-day destination. Options include the 15th-century Mosteiro dos Jerónimos and Torre de Belém, created to wave off the country's expeditions of discovery, as well as the Museu Nacional dos Coches (see page 98) in its two very different settings.
mosteirojeronimos.pt; torrebelem.pt; museudoscoches.pt

Best events
What to see

01 Trienal de Arquitectura de Lisboa: Experimental but accessible, the Trienal takes place at venues across the city with projects by local and international architects.
Every three years, trienaldelisboa.com

02 Dia da Liberdade: Live music and other free events to celebrate the country's revolution against the Salazar dictatorship in 1974.
25 April

03 Arco Lisboa: Lisbon's contemporary-art fair with a focus on local artists.
May, ifema.es/arcolisboa_06

04 IndieLisboa: This 12-day film festival features independent films from Portugal and abroad, talks by film-makers and critics, plus seminars and debates.
May, indielisboa.com

05 Festival de Sintra: Annual classical-music festival in the beautiful parks, gardens and palaces in and around Sintra.
May, festivaldesintra.pt

06 Festa do Santo António: Celebrating Lisbon's patron saint with grilled sardines, live music, parades and all-night street parties.
12-13 June

07 Experimenta Design: Biennial celebration of Portuguese and international design with conferences, exhibitions and workshops.
Autumn/winter, experimentadesign.pt

08 Outfest: Music festival in Barreiro that features bands from around the world.
October, outfest.pt

09 DocLisboa: Documentary film festival. Films are shown in their original languages with Portuguese subtitles.
19-29 October, doclisboa.org

10 Web Summit: For four days, 60,000 self-professed geeks descend on Lisbon for this technology conference.
6-9 November, websummit.com

About Monocle
—— Step inside

In 2007, Monocle was launched as a monthly magazine briefing on global affairs, business, culture, design and much more. We believed there was a globally minded audience of readers who were hungry for opportunities and experiences beyond their national borders.

Today Monocle is a complete media brand with print, audio and online elements – not to mention our expanding network of shops and cafés. Besides our London HQ we have six international bureaux in New York, Toronto, Singapore, Tokyo, Zürich and Hong Kong. We continue to grow and flourish and at our core is the simple belief that there will always be a place for a print brand that is committed to telling fresh stories and sending photographers on assignments. It's also a case of knowing that our success is all down to the readers, advertisers and collaborators who have supported us along the way.

London HQ
—
Our editorial office is in Marylebone

❶
International bureaux
Boots on the ground

We have an HQ in London and call upon firsthand reports from our contributors in more than 35 cities around the world. We also have six international bureaux. For this travel guide, MONOCLE reporters Chloë Ashby, Joe Pickard and Carlota Rebelo decamped to Lisbon to explore all that it has to offer. They also called on the assistance of writers in the city, as well as our correspondent Trish Lorenz, to ensure that we have covered the best in retail, food, hospitality and entertainment. The aim is to make you, the reader, feel like a local when visiting the Portuguese capital.

❷
Online
Digital delivery

We have a dynamic website: *monocle.com*. As well as being the place to hear our radio station, Monocle 24, the site presents our films, which are beautifully shot and edited by our in-house team and provide a fresh perspective on our stories. Check out the films celebrating the cities that make up our Travel Guide Series before you explore the rest of the site.

❸
Retail and cafés
Food for thought

Via our shops in Hong Kong, Toronto, New York, Tokyo, London and Singapore we sell products that cater to our readers' tastes and are produced in collaboration with brands that we believe in. We also have cafés in Tokyo and London. And if you are in the UK capital visit the Kioskafé in Paddington, which combines good coffee and great reads.

④
Print
Committed to the page

MONOCLE is published 10 times
a year. We have stayed loyal to our
belief in quality print with two extra
seasonal publications: THE FORECAST,
packed with key insights into the
year ahead, and THE ESCAPIST, our
summer travel-minded magazine. To
sign up visit *monocle.com/subscribe*.
Since 2013 we have also been
publishing books, like this one,
in partnership with Gestalten.

⑤
Radio
Sound approach

Monocle 24 is our round-the-
clock radio station that was
launched in 2011. It delivers
global news and shows covering
foreign affairs, urbanism, business,
culture, food and drink, design
and print media. When you find
yourself in Lisbon tune into
The Globalist, our morning news
programme that is the perfect way
to start the day in Europe. We also
have a playlist to accompany you
day and night, regularly assisted
by live band sessions that are
hosted at our Midori House
headquarters in London. You
can listen live or download any
of our shows from *monocle.com*,
iTunes or SoundCloud.

Priority service
Subscribers
save 10 per
cent in our
online shop

Join the club

01
Subscribe to Monocle
A subscription is a simple
way to make sure that
you never miss an issue
– and you'll enjoy many
additional benefits.

02
Be in the know
Our subscribers have
exclusive access to the
entire Monocle archive, and
priority access to selected
product collaborations, at
monocle.com.

03
Stay in the loop
Subscription copies are
delivered to your door at no
extra cost no matter where
you are in the world. We also
offer an auto-renewal service
to ensure that you never
miss an issue.

04
And there's more...
Subscribers benefit from a
10 per cent discount at all
Monocle shops, including
online, and receive exclusive
offers and invitations to
events around the world.

Choose your package

Premium one year
12 × issues
+ Porter Sub Club bag

One year
12 × issues
+ Monocle Voyage tote bag

Six months
6 × issues

Chief photographer
Pedro Guimaraes

Photography assistant
Fábio Cunha

Still life
David Sykes

Photographer
Rodrigo Cardoso

Writers
Chloë Ashby
Yasmine Awwad
Mariana Duarte Silva
Josh Fehnert
Luís Leal Miranda
Joe Lloyd
Trish Lorenz
Anja Mutic
Tiago Pais
Joe Pickard
Dan Poole
Carlota Rebelo
Pedro Santos Guerreiro
Joana Stichini Vilela
Syma Tariq
Anna Winston

Images
Alamy
Juan Baraja
Paulo Coelho
Hufton+Crow
Márcia Lessa
Bruno Lopes
Vera Marmelo
Francisco Nogueira
Sanda Pagaimo
Daniel Viana Martins

Illustrators
Satoshi Hashimoto
Ceylan Sahin Eker
Tokuma

Monocle
EDITOR IN CHIEF AND CHAIRMAN
Tyler Brûlé
EDITOR
Andrew Tuck
CREATIVE DIRECTOR
Richard Spencer Powell

The Monocle Travel Guide Series: Lisbon
GUIDE EDITOR
Chloë Ashby
ASSOCIATE GUIDE EDITORS
Joe Pickard
Carlota Rebelo
PHOTO EDITOR
Victoria Cagol

The Monocle Travel Guide Series
SERIES EDITOR
Joe Pickard
ASSOCIATE EDITOR
Chloë Ashby
ASSISTANT EDITOR
Mikaela Aitken
RESEARCHER
Melkon Charchoglyan
DESIGNER
Loi Xuan Ly
PHOTO EDITORS
Matthew Beaman
Shin Miura
Victoria Cagol

PRODUCTION
Jacqueline Deacon
Dan Poole
Rachel Kurzfield
Sean McGeady
Sonia Zhuravlyova

CHAPTER EDITING

Need to know
Trish Lorenz

Hotels
Chloë Ashby

Food and drink
Trish Lorenz

Retail
Chloë Ashby
Joe Pickard
Carlota Rebelo

Things we'd buy
Joe Pickard
Carlota Rebelo

Essays
Chloë Ashby

Culture
Chloë Ashby

Design and architecture
Joe Pickard
Joe Lloyd

Sport and fitness
Chloë Ashby

Walks
Chloë Ashby

Resources
Trish Lorenz

Research
Beatrice Carmi
Melkon Charchoglyan
Arabel Charlaff
Daphne Karnezis
Fabian Mayer
Charles McFarlane
Kristian Radev
Paige Reynolds
Aliz Tennant

Special thanks
Kathy Ball
Pedro Beça
Miguel Coutinho
Pete Kempshall
Nick Mee
Turismo de Lisboa

A

A Carioca, *Bairro Alto* 44
A Cevicheria, *Bairro Alto* 30
A Provinciana, *Liberdade e
 Castilho* 39
A Vida Portuguesa, *Anjos* 49
Acqua Lisboa City Spa, *Avenidas
 Novas* 126
Água no Bico, *Santa Catarina* 37
Alcântara 47, 53, 55, 60, 98, 118
Alfama 23, 43, 58, 122, 126,
 136 – 137
Aloha Café, *Príncipe Real* 37
Altis Belém Hotel & Spa,
 Belém 19
Anjos 30, 49, 54, 123
Antigo Hotel Vitória, *Liberdade
 e Castilho* 121
Antónia Petiscos, *Bairro Alto* 32
Ao 26 Vegan Food Project,
 Chiado 37
Atelier-Museu Júlio Pomar, *São
 Bento* 98
Avenidas Novas 19, 33, 34, 39,
 54, 95, 113, 119, 120, 124, 126

B

Bairro Alto 21, 24, 30, 32, 37, 39,
 44, 45, 46, 50, 63, 104, 105
Bairro do Avillez, *Chiado* 29
Baixa 20 – 21, 26, 31, 33, 43, 50,
 96, 104, 122, 123, 126
Baixa House, *Baixa* 20 – 21
Barbearia Campos,
 Chiado 126
Barbearia Oliveira, *Alfama* 126
Belcanto, *Chiado* 39
Belém 19, 31, 94, 96, 98, 102,
 111, 112 – 113, 120, 121, 124
Bica 104
Bica do Sapato, *São Vicente* 35
Bistro 100 Maneiras, *Chiado* 33
BSpas by Karin Herzog,
 Belém 124
Burel Mountain Originals,
 Chiado 52

C

Café A Brasileira, *Chiado* 42
Café com Calma, *Marvila* 42
Café Lisboa, *Chiado* 32
Café Tati, *Cais do Sodré* 40
Cais do Sodré 37, 38, 40, 44, 47,
 104, 114
Campo de Ourique 44, 100,
 130 – 131
Campo Grande 96, 100
Campolide 104, 113, 120
Cantinho do Aziz, *Mouraria* 37
Caroline Pagès Gallery, *Campo
 de Ourique* 100
Casa C'Alma, *Príncipe Real* 16
Casa da Índia, *Bairro Alto* 39

Casa das Bifanas, *Baixa* 33
Casa das Histórias, *Cascais* 116
Casa dos Bicos, *Alfama* 122
Casa Pau-Brasil, *Príncipe Real* 57
Casa-Museu Medeiros e Almeida,
 Liberdade e Castilho 98
Cascais 116
Castelo 22
Caza das Vellas Loreto,
 Bairro Alto 50
Centro Cultural de Belém,
 Belém 102
Cervejaria Liberdade,
 Liberdade e Castilho 34
Cervejaria Ramiro, *Anjos* 30
Chapelarias Azevedo Rua,
 Baixa 50
Chiado 29, 32, 33, 36, 37, 39, 40,
 42, 48, 50, 52, 53, 56, 59, 60,
 61, 63, 65, 97, 105, 126
Cinco Lounge, *Príncipe Real* 46
Cinema Ideal, *Bairro Alto* 105
Cinema São Jorge, *Liberdade e
 Castilho* 106
Cinemateca Portuguesa,
 Liberdade e Castilho 106
CitySpa, *Restelo* 125
Claus Porto, *Chiado* 48, 126
Companhia Portugueza do Chá,
 Santos 44
Conserveira de Lisboa,
 Alfama 43
Copenhagen Coffee Lab, *Príncipe
 Real* 42
Cortiço & Netos, *Graça* 51
Cristina Guerra Contemporary
 Art, *Estrela e Lapa* 100
Cristina Jorge de Carvalho,
 Liberdade e Castilho 64
Culturgest, *Roma e Areeiro* 103
Cutipol, *Chiado* 65

D

Damas, *Graça* 104

E

Elevador de Santa Justa,
 Baixa 122
Embaixada, *Príncipe Real* 58
Energias de Portugal HQ,
 Cais do Sodré 114
Espaço B, *Príncipe Real* 62
Espaço Espelho d'Água,
 Belém 120
Espaço Mínimo, *Chiado* 65
Essays 69 – 92
Estrela e Lapa 65, 100

F

Fábrica Braço de Prata,
 Marvila 102
Fábrica de Cerâmica da Viúva
 Lamego, *Anjos* 123

Fabrica Features, *Chiado* 56
Feeting Room, The, *Chiado* 59
Fern, *Bairro Alto* 63
Figaro's, *Chiado* 126
Flur, *São Vicente* 54
Fora, *Chiado* 50
Four Seasons Hotel Ritz Spa,
 The, *Avenidas Novas* 124
Fundação Champalimaud,
 Belém 111

G

Galeria Francisco Fino,
 Marvila 99
Galeria Madragoa, *Santos* 99
Galeria 111, *Campo Grande* 100
Galeria Pedro Cera, *Campo de
 Ourique* 100
Galeria Tereza Seabra, *Bairro
 Alto* 63
Galeria 3 + 1, *São Bento* 101
Galeria Zé dos Bois, *Bairro
 Alto* 104
Galerias de São Bento, *São
 Bento* 59
Galeto, *Avenidas Novas* 33
Gambrinus, *Liberdade e
 Castilho* 28
Gare do Oriente, *Parque das
 Nações* 117
Garrafeira Alfaia, *Bairro Alto* 44
Ginjinha Sem Rival,
 Liberdade e Castilho 47
Graça 18 – 19, 51, 104
GS1 HQ, *Lumiar* 114
Gulbenkian Café, *Avenidas
 Novas* 34

H

Heim Café, *Santos* 40
Hello, Kristof, *Santa Catarina* 41
Hotel White Lisboa, *Avenidas
 Novas* 19

I

Ibo, *Cais do Sodré* 37
Icon, *Chiado* 56
Igreja de Nossa Senhora
 Auxiliadora, *Prazeres* 118
Impasse, *Liberdade e
 Castilho* 62
Independente Suites and Terrace,
 The, *Bairro Alto* 21
Insólito, The, *Bairro Alto* 46

J

Jesus é Goês, *Liberdade e
 Castilho* 31

K

Kolovrat 79, *Príncipe Real* 61

L

La Boulangerie, *Prazeres* 39
Late Birds Lisbon, The, *Bairro Alto* 24
Laurentina, *Avenidas Novas* 34
Less, *Príncipe Real* 35
Liberdade e Castilho 27, 28, 31, 34, 39, 46, 47, 61, 62, 64, 98, 106, 121
Livraria Artes e Letras, *São Bento* 51
Livraria Ferin, *Chiado* 53
Livraria Ler Devagar, *Alcântara* 55
Lounge, *Bica* 104
Lumiar 114
Luvaria Ulisses, *Chiado* 52
LX Factory, *Alcântara* 60

M

Maat, *Belém* 94, 112 – 113
Maison Nuno Gama, *Príncipe Real* 62
Manteigaria Silva, *Baixa* 43
Margarida Fabrica, *Alcântara* 53
Marvila 42, 99, 101, 102, 132 – 133
Memmo Alfama, *Alfama* 23
Memmo Príncipe Real, *Príncipe Real* 24 – 25
Meo Arena, *Parque das Nações* 116
Mercado da Ribeira, *Cais do Sodré* 44
Mercado de Campo de Ourique, *Campo de Ourique* 44
Metrostudio, *Baixa* 126
Micasaenlisboa, *Graça* 18 – 19
Mini by Luna, *Príncipe Real* 60
Mouraria 37, 39, 46, 128 – 129
Mude, *Baixa* 96
Museu Calouste Gulbenkian, *Avenidas Novas* 95, 119
Museu Coleção Berardo, *Belém* 96
Museu do Oriente, *Alcântara* 98
Museu Nacional de Arte Antiga, *Santos* 97
Museu Nacional de Arte Contemporânea do Chiado, *Chiado* 97
Museu Nacional do Azulejo, *São João* 93
Museu Nacional dos Coches, *Belém* 98
Museu Rafael Bordalo Pinheiro, *Campo Grande* 96
Music Box, *Cais do Sodré* 104

N

Need to know 14 – 15

O

O Apartamento 102
O Talho, *Avenidas Novas* 39
Óptica do Sacramento, *Chiado* 52

P

Padrão dos Descobrimentos, *Belém* 121
Palácio Belmonte, *Castelo* 22
Palácio Chiado, *Chiado* 36
Palácio da Justiça, *Avenidas Novas* 120
Palácio Ramalhete, *Santos* 25
Pap'Açorda, *Cais do Sodré* 38
Park Bar, *Bairro Alto* 45
Parque das Nações 115, 116, 117, 134 – 135
Pastéis de Belém, *Belém* 31
Pátria: Arte. Arquitetura. Design, *Estrela e Lapa* 65
Pavilhão Chinês, *Bairro Alto* 46
Pavilhão de Portugal, *Parque das Nações* 115
Pavilhão do Conhecimento, *Parque das Nações* 116
Pensão Amor, *Cais do Sodré* 47
+351, *São Bento* 60
Ponte 25 de Abril, *Alcântara* 118
Pousada de Lisboa, *Baixa* 26
Praça do Comércio, *Baixa* 123
Prazeres 39, 118
Príncipe Real 16, 24 – 25, 35, 37, 42, 43, 46, 52, 57, 58, 60, 61, 62

R

Reitoria da Universidade Nova de Lisboa, *Campolide* 113
Resources 138 – 139
Restaurante Bastardo, *Baixa* 31
Restelo 125
Rio Maravilha, *Alcântara* 47
Rive Rouge, *Cais do Sodré* 47
Roma e Areeiro 103
Rosa & Teixeira, *Liberdade e Castilho* 61

S

Sal Concept Store, *Santa Catarina* 64
Santa Catarina 32, 37, 41, 64
Santa Clara 1728, *São Vicente* 17
Santos 25, 26, 40, 44, 97, 99
São Bento 51, 59, 60, 98, 101
São João 93
São Luiz Teatro Municipal, *Chiado* 105
São Vicente 17, 35, 54
Sapataria do Carmo, *Chiado* 60
Sea Me Peixaria Moderna, *Bairro Alto* 30
Sky Bar, *Liberdade e Castilho* 46
Slou, *Chiado* 61

Solar Tiles, *Príncipe Real* 52
Stone Block, *Avenidas Novas* 113

T

Taberna Portuguesa, *Santa Catarina* 32
Tapisco, *Bairro Alto* 37
Tartine, *Chiado* 40
Tease Café, *Príncipe Real* 43
Teatro Aberto, *Campolide* 104
Teatro do Bairro, *Bairro Alto* 105
Teatro Nacional Dona Maria II, *Baixa* 104
Teresa Pavão, *Alfama* 58
Terra, *Príncipe Real* 37
Things we'd buy 66 – 68
Topo, *Mouraria* 46
Torres das Amoreiras, *Campolide* 120
266 Avenida da Liberdade, *Liberdade e Castilho* 121

U

Under the Cover, *Avenidas Novas* 54
Underdogs Gallery, *Marvila* 101

V

Valverde Hotel, *Liberdade e Castilho* 27
Véronique Boutique, *Chiado* 63
Verso Branco, *Santa Catarina* 64

X

XYZ Books, *Anjos* 54

Y

York House Lisboa, *Santos* 26

Z

Zé da Mouraria, *Mouraria* 39

Right, where next?

❶ **London**

❷ **New York**

❸ **Tokyo**

❹ **Hong Kong**

❺ **Madrid**

❻ **Bangkok**

❼ **Istanbul**

❽ **Miami**

❾ **Rio de Janeiro**

❿ **Paris**

⓫ **Singapore**

⓬ **Vienna**

⓭ **Sydney**

⓮ **Honolulu**

⓯ **Copenhagen**

⓰ **Los Angeles**

⓱ **Toronto**

⓲ **Berlin**

⓳ **Rome**

⓴ **Venice**

㉑ **Amsterdam**

㉒ **Stockholm**

㉓ **Lisbon**